Modern Critical Interpretations

Samuel Beckett's
Endgame

Modern Critical Interpretations

The Oresteia
Beowulf
The General Prologue to
   The Canterbury Tales
The Pardoner's Tale
The Knight's Tale
The Divine Comedy
Exodus
Genesis
The Gospels
The Iliad
The Book of Job
Volpone
Doctor Faustus
The Revelation of St.
   John the Divine
The Song of Songs
Oedipus Rex
The Aeneid
The Duchess of Malfi
Antony and Cleopatra
As You Like It
Coriolanus
Hamlet
Henry IV, Part I
Henry IV, Part II
Henry V
Julius Caesar
King Lear
Macbeth
Measure for Measure
The Merchant of Venice
A Midsummer Night's
   Dream
Much Ado About
   Nothing
Othello
Richard II
Richard III
The Sonnets
Taming of the Shrew
The Tempest
Twelfth Night
The Winter's Tale
Emma
Mansfield Park
Pride and Prejudice
The Life of Samuel
   Johnson
Moll Flanders
Robinson Crusoe
Tom Jones
The Beggar's Opera
Gray's Elegy
Paradise Lost
The Rape of the Lock
Tristram Shandy
Gulliver's Travels

Evelina
The Marriage of Heaven
   and Hell
Songs of Innocence and
   Experience
Jane Eyre
Wuthering Heights
Don Juan
The Rime of the Ancient
   Mariner
Bleak House
David Copperfield
Hard Times
A Tale of Two Cities
Middlemarch
The Mill on the Floss
Jude the Obscure
The Mayor of
   Casterbridge
The Return of the Native
Tess of the D'Urbervilles
The Odes of Keats
Frankenstein
Vanity Fair
Barchester Towers
The Prelude
The Red Badge of
   Courage
The Scarlet Letter
The Ambassadors
Daisy Miller, The Turn
   of the Screw, and
   Other Tales
The Portrait of a Lady
Billy Budd, Benito Cer-
   eno, Bartleby the Scriv-
   ener, and Other Tales
Moby-Dick
The Tales of Poe
Walden
Adventures of
   Huckleberry Finn
The Life of Frederick
   Douglass
Heart of Darkness
Lord Jim
Nostromo
A Passage to India
Dubliners
A Portrait of the Artist as
   a Young Man
Ulysses
Kim
The Rainbow
Sons and Lovers
Women in Love
1984
Major Barbara

Man and Superman
Pygmalion
St. Joan
The Playboy of the
   Western World
The Importance of Being
   Earnest
Mrs. Dalloway
To the Lighthouse
My Antonia
An American Tragedy
Murder in the Cathedral
The Waste Land
Absalom, Absalom!
Light in August
Sanctuary
The Sound and the Fury
The Great Gatsby
A Farewell to Arms
The Sun Also Rises
Arrowsmith
Lolita
The Iceman Cometh
Long Day's Journey Into
   Night
The Grapes of Wrath
Miss Lonelyhearts
The Glass Menagerie
A Streetcar Named
   Desire
Their Eyes Were
   Watching God
Native Son
Waiting for Godot
Herzog
All My Sons
Death of a Salesman
Gravity's Rainbow
All the King's Men
The Left Hand of
   Darkness
The Brothers Karamazov
Crime and Punishment
Madame Bovary
The Interpretation of
   Dreams
The Castle
The Metamorphosis
The Trial
Man's Fate
The Magic Mountain
Montaigne's Essays
Remembrance of Things
   Past
The Red and the Black
Anna Karenina
War and Peace

These and other titles in preparation

Modern Critical Interpretations

Samuel Beckett's
Endgame

Edited and with an introduction by
Harold Bloom
Sterling Professor of the Humanities
Yale University

Chelsea House Publishers ◇ *1988*
NEW YORK ◇ NEW HAVEN ◇ PHILADELPHIA

© 1988 by Chelsea House Publishers, a division
of Chelsea House Educational Communications, Inc.,
   345 Whitney Avenue, New Haven, CT 06511
   95 Madison Avenue, New York, NY 10016
   5068B West Chester Pike, Edgemont, PA 19028

Introduction © 1988 by Harold Bloom

Printed and bound in the United States of America

10 9 8 7 6 5 4 3 2 1

∞ The paper used in this publication meets the minimum
requirements of the American National Standard for
Permanence of Paper for Printed Library Materials,
Z39.48-1984.

Library of Congress Cataloging-in-Publication Data
Samuel Beckett's Endgame.
   (Modern critical interpretations)
   Bibliography: p.
   Includes index.
   I. Beckett, Samuel, 1906–   . Fin de partie.
I. Bloom, Harold.   II. Series.
PQ2603.E378F5867   1988   842'.914   87–15791
ISBN 1–55546–056–9 (alk. paper)

Contents

Editor's Note

This book brings together a representative selection of the best critical interpretations of Samuel Beckett's masterpiece, the drama *Endgame*. The critical essays are reprinted here in the chronological order of their original publication. I am grateful to Edward Jefferson for his assistance in editing this volume.

My introduction meditates upon *Endgame* as a kind of play-within-a-play, and speculates as to the status of the enclosing play, as it were. The distinguished Frankfurt theorist Theodor W. Adorno begins the chronological sequence of criticism with his mordant discussion of how *Endgame* reduces the possibility of a philosophy like Existentialism to "culture-trash."

Hugh Kenner, possibly Beckett's foremost exegete, emphasizes the play's sense of itself as self-conscious performance and chess match, and finds this to be a saving theatricality. In Antony Easthope's view, *Endgame*'s dramatic method juxtaposes a formal surface of ironic repartee with the authentic depth of Hamm's "chronicle."

The philosopher Stanley Cavell examines Beckett's uses of literality and the philosophical questions the play's "hidden literality" asks, particularly about Hamm's Noah-like predicament.

Like Adorno, Richard Gilman rejects weak misreadings of *Endgame* as Existentialist philosophy, and sees it instead as depicting the self-dramatizing ways through which we fill the void. An analysis of the play's language by Paul Lawley shows that it, despite extreme stylization, resonates with mythic connotations.

Studying the drafts of *Endgame,* the eminent Beckett scholar Ruby Cohn illustrates how the revisions produced more consistency of details, symmetrical characters, and sustained themes. In this book's final essay, Sidney Homan focuses upon the heroic aspects of Hamm as an artist, and clarifies the complementary roles of Clov, Nagg, and Nell.

Introduction

Jonathan Swift, so much the strongest ironist in the language as to have no rivals, wrote the prose masterpiece of the language in *A Tale of a Tub*. Samuel Beckett, as much the legitimate descendant of Swift as he is of his friend, James Joyce, has written the prose masterpieces of the language in this century, sometimes as translations from his own French originals. Such an assertion does not discount the baroque splendors of *Ulysses* and *Finnegans Wake*, but prefers to them the purity of *Murphy* and *Watt*, and of Beckett's renderings into English of *Malone Dies*, *The Unnamable* and *How It Is*. Unlike Swift and Joyce, Beckett is only secondarily an ironist and, despite his brilliance at tragicomedy, is something other than a comic writer. His Cartesian dualism seems to me less fundamental than his profoundly Schopenhauerian vision. Perhaps Swift, had he read and tolerated Schopenhauer, might have turned into Beckett.

A remarkable number of the greatest novelists have found Schopenhauer more than congenial: one thinks of Turgenev, Tolstoy, Zola, Hardy, Conrad, Thomas Mann, even of Proust. As those seven novelists have in common only the activity of writing novels, we may suspect that Schopenhauer's really horrifying system helps a novelist to do his work. This is not to discount the intellectual and spiritual persuasiveness of Schopenhauer. A philosopher who so deeply affected Wagner, Nietzsche, Wittgenstein and (despite his denials) Freud, hardly can be regarded only as a convenient aid to storytellers and storytelling. Nevertheless, Schopenhauer evidently stimulated the arts of fiction, but why? Certain it is that we cannot read *The World as Will and Representation* as a work of fiction. Who could bear it as fiction? Supplementing his book, Schopenhauer characterizes the Will to Live:

> Here also life presents itself by no means as a gift for enjoyment,
> but as a task, a drudgery to be performed; and in accordance

> with this we see, in great and small, universal need, ceaseless
> cares, constant pressure, endless strife, compulsory activity, with
> extreme exertion of all the powers of body and mind. . . . All
> strive, some planning, others acting; the tumult is indescribable.
> But the ultimate aim of it all, what is it? To sustain ephemeral
> and tormented individuals through a short span of time in the
> most fortunate case with endurable want and comparative free-
> dom from pain, which, however, is at once attended with ennui;
> then the reproduction of this race and its striving. In this evident
> disproportion between the trouble and the reward, the will to
> live appears to us from this point of view, if taken objectively,
> as a fool, or subjectively, as a delusion, seized by which every-
> thing living works with the utmost exertion of its strength for
> something that is of no value. But when we consider it more
> closely, we shall find here also that it is rather a blind pressure,
> a tendency entirely without ground or motive.

Hugh Kenner suggests that Beckett reads Descartes as fiction. Beckett's
fiction suggests that Beckett reads Schopenhauer as truth. Descartes as a
precursor is safely distant; Joyce was much too close, and *Murphy* and even
Watt are Joycean books. Doubtless, Beckett turned to French in *Molloy* so
as to exorcise Joyce, and certainly, from *Malone Dies* on, the prose when
translated back into English has ceased to be Joycean. Joyce is to Beckett
as Milton was to Wordsworth. *Finnegans Wake,* like *Paradise Lost,* is a
triumph demanding study; Beckett's trilogy, like *The Prelude,* internalizes
the triumph by way of the compensatory imagination, in which experience
and loss become one. Study does little to unriddle Beckett or Wordsworth.
The Old Cumberland Beggar, Michael, Margaret of *The Ruined Cottage;*
these resist analysis as do Molloy, Malone, and the Unnamable. Place my
namesake, the sublime Poldy, in *Murphy* and he might fit, though he would
explode the book. Place him in *Watt?* It cannot be done, and Poldy (or even
Earwicker) in the trilogy would be like Milton (or Satan) perambulating
about in *The Prelude.*

The fashion (largely derived from French misreaders of German
thought) of denying a fixed, stable ego is a shibboleth of current criticism.
But such a denial is precisely like each literary generation's assertion that
it truly writes the common language rather than a poetic diction. Both
stances define modernism, and modernism is as old as Hellenistic Alex-
andria. Callimachus is as modernist as Joyce, and Aristarchus, like Hugh
Kenner, is an antiquarian modernist or modernist antiquarian. Schopen-

hauer dismissed the ego as an illusion, life as torment, and the universe as nothing, and he rightly credited these insights to that great modernist, the Buddha. Beckett too is as modernist as the Buddha, or as Schopenhauer, who disputes with Hume the position of the best writer among philosophers since Plato. I laugh sometimes in reading Schopenhauer, but the laughter is defensive. Beckett provokes laughter, as Falstaff does, or in the mode of Shakespeare's clowns.

II

In his early monograph, *Proust,* Beckett cites Schopenhauer's definition of the artistic procedure as "the contemplation of the world independently of the principle of reason." Such more-than-rational contemplation gives Proust those Ruskinian or Paterian privileged moments that are "epiphanies" in Joyce but which Beckett mordantly calls "fetishes" in Proust. Transcendental bursts of radiance necessarily are no part of Beckett's cosmos, which resembles, if anything at all, the Demiurge's creation in ancient Gnosticism. Basilides or Valentinus, Alexandrian heresiarchs, would have recognized instantly the world of the trilogy and of the major plays: *Waiting for Godot, Endgame, Krapp's Last Tape.* It is the world ruled by the Archons, the *kenoma,* nonplace of emptiness. Beckett's enigmatic spirituality quests, though sporadically, for a void that is a fulness, the Abyss or *pleroma* that the Gnostics called both forefather and foremother. Call this a natural rather than a revealed Gnosticism in Beckett's case, but Gnosticism it is nevertheless. Schopenhauer's quietism is at last not Beckett's, which is to say that for Beckett, as for Blake and for the Gnostics, the Creation and the Fall were the same event.

The young Beckett, bitterly reviewing a translation of Rilke into English, memorably rejected Rilke's transcendental self-deceptions, where the poet mistook his own tropes as spiritual evidences:

> Such a turmoil of self-deception and naif discontent gains nothing in dignity from that prime article of the Rilkean faith, which provides for the interchangeability of Rilke and God. . . . He has the fidgets, a disorder which may very well give rise, as it did with Rilke on occasion, to poetry of a high order. But why call the fidgets God, Ego, Orpheus, and the rest?

In 1938, the year that *Murphy* was belatedly published, Beckett declared his double impatience with the language of transcendence and with the transcendence of language, while intimating also the imminence of the swerve away from Joyce in the composition of *Watt* (1942–44):

> At first it can only be a matter of somehow finding a method by which we can represent this mocking attitude towards the word, through words. In this dissonance between the means and their use it will perhaps become possible to feel a whisper of that final music or that silence that underlies All.
>
> With such a program, in my opinion, the latest work of Joyce has nothing whatever to do. There it seems rather to be a matter of an apotheosis of the word. Unless perhaps Ascension to Heaven and Descent to Hell are somehow one and the same.

As a Gnostic imagination, Beckett's way is Descent, in what cannot be called a hope to liberate the sparks imprisoned in words. Hope is alien to Beckett's mature fiction, so that we can say its images are Gnostic but not its program, since it lacks all program. A Gnosticism without potential transcendence is the most negative of all possible negative stances, and doubtless accounts for the sympathetic reader's sense that every crucial work by Beckett necessarily must be his last. Yet the grand paradox is that lessness never ends in Beckett.

III

"Nothing is got for nothing." That is the later version of Emerson's law of Compensation, in the essay "Power" of *The Conduct of Life*. Nothing is got for nothing even in Beckett, this greatest master of nothing. In the progression from *Murphy* through *Watt* and the trilogy on to *How It Is* and the briefer fictions of recent years, there is loss for the reader as well as gain. The same is true of the movement from *Godot*, *Endgame*, and *Krapp's Last Tape* down to the short plays of Beckett's current and perhaps final phase. A wild humor abandons Beckett, or is transformed into a comedy for which we seem not to be ready. Even an uncommon reader can long for those marvelous Pythagoreans, Wylie and Neary, who are the delight of *Murphy*, or for the sense of the picturesque that makes a last stand in *Molloy*. Though the mode was Joyce's, the music of Wylie and Neary is Beckett's alone:

> "These are dark sayings," said Wylie.
> Neary turned his cup upside down.
> "Needle," he said, "as it is with the love of the body, so with

the friendship of the mind, the full is only reached by admittance
to the most retired places. Here are the pudenda of my psyche."

"Cathleen," cried Wylie.

"But betray me," said Neary, "and you go the way of
Hippasos."

"The Adkousmatic, I presume," said Wylie. "His retribution
slips my mind."

"Drowned in a puddle," said Neary, "for having divulged
the incommensurability of side and diagonal."

"So perish all babblers," said Wylie. . . .

"Do not quibble," said Neary harshly. "You saved my life.
Now palliate it."

"I greatly fear," said Wylie, "that the syndrome known as
life is too diffuse to admit of palliation. For every symptom that
is eased, another is made worse. The horse leech's daughter is
a closed system. Her quantum of wantum cannot vary."

"Very prettily put," said Neary.

One can be forgiven for missing this, even as one surrenders these
easier pleasures for the more difficult pleasures of How It Is:

my life above what I did in my life above a little of everything
tried everything then gave up no worse always a hole a ruin
always a crust never any good at anything not made for that
farrago too complicated crawl about in corners and sleep all I
wanted I got it nothing left but go to heaven

The Sublime mode, according to a great theorist, Angus Fletcher, has
"the direct and serious function of destroying the slavery of pleasure."
Beckett is certainly the strongest Western author living in the year 1987,
the last survivor of the sequence that includes Proust, Kafka, and Joyce. It
seems odd to name Beckett, most astonishing of minimalists, as a representative of the Sublime mode, but the isolation and terror of the High
Sublime return in the catastrophe creations of Beckett, in that vision Fletcher
calls "catastrophe as a gradual grinding down and slowing to a dead stop."
A Sublime that moves towards silence necessarily relies upon a rhetoric of
waning lyricism, in which the entire scale of effects is transformed. As John
Hollander notes:

Sentences, phrases, images even, are the veritable arias in the
plays and the later fiction. The magnificent rising of the kite at

the end of *Murphy* occurs in a guarded but positive surge of ceremonial song, to which he will never return.

Kafka's Hunter Gracchus, who had been glad to live and was glad to die, tells us that: "I slipped into my winding sheet like a girl into her marriage dress. I lay and waited. Then came the mishap." The mishap, a moment's error on the part of the death-ship's pilot, moves Gracchus from the heroic world of romance to the world of Kafka and of Beckett, where one is neither alive nor dead. It is Beckett's peculiar triumph that he disputes with Kafka the dark eminence of being the Dante of that world. Only Kafka, or Beckett, could have written the sentence in which Gracchus sums up the dreadfulness of his condition: "The thought of helping me is an illness that has to be cured by taking to one's bed." Murphy might have said that; Malone is beyond saying anything so merely expressionistic. The "beyond" is where Beckett's later fictions and plays reside. Call it the silence, or the abyss, or the reality beyond the pleasure principle, or the metaphysical or spiritual reality of our existence at last exposed, beyond further illusion. Beckett cannot or will not name it, but he has worked through to the art of representing it more persuasively than anyone else.

IV

Trying to understand *Endgame,* Theodor W. Adorno attained to a most somber conclusion:

> Consciousness begins to look its own demise in the eye, as if it wanted to survive the demise, as these two want to survive the destruction of their world. Proust, about whom the young Beckett wrote an essay, is said to have attempted to keep protocol on his own struggle with death. . . . *Endgame* carries out this intention like a mandate from a testament.

Hugh Kenner, a very different ideologue than Adorno, was less somber: "The despair in which he traffics is a conviction, not a philosophy." A reader and playgoer who, like myself, enjoys *Endgame* more than any other stage drama of this century, may wish to dissent from both Adorno and Kenner. Neither the struggle with death nor the conviction of despair seems to me central in the play. An extraordinary gusto informs *Endgame,* surpassing even Brecht, Pirandello, and Ionesco in that quality. It is a gusto quite indistinguishable from an acute anxiety attack, but anxiety and anxious expectations need not be confused with despair (or hope) or with a struggle against death. *Endgame* contrives to be both biblical and Shakespearean, despite its customary Schopenhauerian and Gnostic assumptions. Anxiety, Freud noted, is the reaction to the danger of object loss, and Hamm fears losing Clov. Or, as Freud ironically also observes, anxiety after all is only a perception—of possibilities of anxiety.

Hamm, a bad chess player, faces his endgame with a compulsive intensity, so that he is formidable though a blunderer. His name necessarily suggests Ham, who saw the nakedness of his father Noah, and whose son Canaan was cursed into servitude for it. That would make Nagg and Nell into Mr. and Mrs. Noah, which seems not inappropriate, but is sufficient without being altogether necessary, as it were. There is enough of a ruined Hamlet in Hamm to work against the story of Noah's flood, and overtly ("our revels now are ended") a touch of a ruined Prospero also. I tend to vote for Beckett's deepest orientations again. Take away from Schopenhauer his aesthetic Sublime, and from ancient Gnosticism its transcendent if alien god, and you are very close to the cosmos of Beckett's *Endgame*.

As in *Waiting for Godot,* we are back in the *kenoma,* or sensible emptiness, a kind of vast yet dry flood. A bungler in Hamm's own image, doubtless the Demiurge, has created this *kenoma,* written this play, except that Hamm himself may be the Demiurge, the artisan or bad hammer responsible for driving in Clov, Nagg, Nell, and all the other nails (to follow Kenner, but with a Gnostic difference). The drama might be titled *Endgame of the Demiurge* or even *Hamlet's Revenge upon Himself.* Kenner and other exegetes have centered upon a single moment in *Hamlet,* where the prince tells Rosencrantz and Guildenstern what they are not capable of knowing, even after they are told:

HAMLET: Denmark's a prison.

ROSENCRANTZ: Then is the world one.

HAMLET: A goodly one, in which there are many confines, wards, and dungeons, Denmark being one o' th' worst.

ROSENCRANTZ: We think not so, my lord.

HAMLET: Why then 'tis none to you; for there is nothing either good or bad, but thinking makes it so. To me it is a prison.

ROSENCRANTZ: Why then your ambition makes it one. 'Tis too narrow for your mind.

HAMLET: O God, I could be bounded in a nutshell, and count myself a king of infinite space—were it not that I have bad dreams.

(ll. 243–56)

Hamm's world has become a prison, with a single confine, ward, and dungeon, a nutshell reduced from infinite space by the Demiurge's bad dreams. *Endgame* is hardly Hamm's bad dream, but a Kafkan Hamlet could be Hamm, Nagg an amalgam of the ghost and Claudius, Nell a plausible Gertrude, and poor Clov a ruined Horatio. Contaminate Hamlet with Kafka's "The Hunter Gracchus," and you might get *Endgame*. Schopenhauer's dreadful Will to Live goes on ravening in Hamm, Clov, Nagg, and Nell, as it must in any dramatic representation, since there can be no mimesis without appetite. Where the Will to Live is unchecked, there are anxious expectations, and anxiety or Hamm is king, but a king on a board swept nearly bare. Kenner thinks Clov a knight and Hamm's parents pawns, but they seem to me out of the game, or taken already. But that raises the authentic aesthetic puzzle of *Endgame*. Is there another, an opposing side, with a rival king, or is there only Hamm, a perfect solipsist where even Hamlet was an imperfect one?

I do not think that Hamm lacks an opponent, since his solipsism is not perfect, hence his anxiety as to losing Clov. The Demiurge, like every bad actor, finds his opponent in the audience, which comes to be beguiled but stays to criticize. Kafka, with high deliberation, wrote so as to make interpretation impossible, but that only displaces what needs interpretation into the question of Kafka's evasiveness. Beckett does not evade; *Endgame* is his masterpiece, and being so inward it is also his most difficult work, with every allusion endstopped, despite the reverberations. There is no play in *Endgame*; it is all Hamlet's *Mousetrap*, or Hamm's. We have only a play-within-a-play, which gives us the difficulty of asking and answering: what then is the play that contains *Endgame?* If the audience is the opponent, and Hamm is bound to lose the endgame, then the enclosing play is the larger entity that can contain the chess game between Hamm and ourselves. That is not quite the play of the world, yet it remains a larger play than any other dramatist has given us in this century.

Trying to Understand *Endgame*

Theodor W. Adorno

Beckett's oeuvre has several elements in common with Parisian existentialism. Reminiscences of the category of "absurdity," of "situation," of "decision" or their opposite permeate it as medieval ruins permeate Kafka's monstrous house on the edge of the city: occasionally, windows fly open and reveal to view the black starless heaven of something like anthropology. But form—conceived by Sartre rather traditionally as that of didactic plays, not at all as something audacious but rather oriented toward an effect—absorbs what is expressed and changes it. Impulses are raised to the level of the most advanced artistic means, those of Joyce and Kafka. Absurdity in Beckett is no longer a state of human existence thinned out to a mere idea and then expressed in images. Poetic procedure surrenders to it without intention. Absurdity is divested of that generality of doctrine which existentialism, that creed of the permanence of individual existence, nonetheless combines with Western pathos of the universal and the immutable. Existential conformity—that one should be what one is—is thereby rejected along with the ease of its representation. What Beckett offers in the way of philosophy he himself also reduces to culture-trash, no different from the innumerable allusions and residues of education which he employs in the wake of the Anglo-Saxon tradition, particularly of Joyce and Eliot. Culture parades before him as the entrails of *Jugendstil* ornaments did before that progress which preceded him, modernism as the obsolescence of the modern. The regressive language demolishes it. Such objectivity in Beckett obliterates the meaning that was culture, along with its rudiments. Culture

From *New German Critique* 26 (Summer 1982). © 1982 by *New German Critique*.

thus begins to fluoresce. He thereby completes a tendency of the recent novel. What was decried as abstract according to the cultural criterion of aesthetic immanence—reflection—is lumped together with pure representation, corroding the Flaubertian principle of the purely self-enclosed matter at hand. The less events can be presumed meaningful in themselves, the more the idea of aesthetic *Gestalt* as a unity of appearance and intention becomes illusory. Beckett relinquishes the illusion by coupling both disparate aspects. Thought becomes as much a means of producing a meaning for the work which cannot be immediately rendered tangible, as it is an expression of meaning's absence. When applied to drama, the word "meaning" is multivalent. It denotes: metaphysical content, which objectively presents itself in the complexion of the artifact; likewise the intention of the whole as a structure of meaning which it signifies in itself; and finally the sense of the words and sentences which the characters speak, and that of their progression—the sense of the dialogue. But these equivocations point toward a common basis. From it, in Beckett's *Endgame,* emerges a continuum. It is historio-philosophically supported by a change in the dramatic a priori: positive metaphysical meaning is no longer possible in such a substantive way (if indeed it ever was), such that dramatic form could have its law in such meaning and its epiphany. Yet that afflicts the form even in its linguistic construction. Drama cannot simply seize on to negative meaning, or its absence, as content, without thereby affecting everything peculiar to it—virtually to the point of reversal to its opposite. What is essential for drama was constituted by that meaning. If drama were to strive to survive meaning aesthetically, it would be reduced to inadequate content or to a clattering machinery demonstrating world views, as often happens in existentialist plays. The explosion of metaphysical meaning, which alone guaranteed the unity of an aesthetic structure of meaning, makes it crumble away with a necessity and stringency which equals that of the transmitted canon of dramaturgical form. Harmonious aesthetic meaning, and certainly its subjectification in a binding tangible intention, substituted for that transcendent meaningfulness, the denial of which itself constituted the content. Through its own organized meaninglessness, the plot must approach that which transpired in the truth content of dramaturgy generally. Such construction of the senseless also even includes linguistic molecules: if they and their connections were rationally meaningful, then within the drama they would synthesize irrevocably into that very meaning structure of the whole which is denied by the whole. The interpretation of *Endgame* therefore cannot chase the chimera of expressing its meaning with the help of philosophical mediation. Understanding it can mean nothing other than understanding its incomprehensibility, or concretely reconstructing its meaning structure—that it has none. Isolated, thought no longer pretends, as the Idea once did, to be itself the structure's meaning—a transcendence which would be engendered and guaranteed by the work's own immanence. Instead, thought transforms itself into a kind of material of a second degree, just as the philosophemes expounded in Thomas Mann's *The Magic Mountain* and *Doctor Faustus,* as novel materials, find their destiny in replacing that sensate immediacy which is diminished in the self-reflective work of art. If such materiality of thought was heretofore largely involuntary, pointing to the dilemma of works which perforce confused themselves with the Idea they could not achieve, then Beckett confronts this challenge and uses thoughts *sans phrase* as phrases, as those material components of the *monologue intérieur* which mind itself has become, the reified residue of education. Whereas pre-Beckett existentialism cannibalized philosophy for poetic purposes as if it were Schiller incarnate, Beckett, as educated as anyone, presents the bill: philosophy, or spirit itself, proclaims its bankruptcy as the dreamlike dross of the experiential world, and the poetic process shows itself as worn out. Disgust (*dégoût*), a productive force in the arts since Baudelaire, is insatiable in Beckett's historically mediated impulses. Everything now impossible becomes canonical, freeing a motif from the prehistory of existentialism—Husserl's universal annihilation of the world—from the shadowy realm of methodology. Totalitarians like Lukács, who rage against the—truly terrifying—simplifier as "decadent," are not ill advised by the interests of their bosses. They hate in Beckett what they have betrayed. Only the nausea of satiation—the tedium of spirit with itself—wants something completely different: prescribed "health" nevertheless makes do with the nourishment offered, with simple fare. Beckett's dégoût cannot be forced to fall in line. He responds to the cheery call to play along with parody, parody of the philosophy spit out by his dialogues as well as parody of forms. Existentialism itself is parodied; nothing remains of its "invariants" other than minimal existence. The drama's opposition to ontology— as the sketch of a first or immutable principle—is unmistakable in an exchange of dialogue which unintentionally garbles Goethe's phrase about "old truths," which has degenerated to an arch-bourgeois sentiment:

> HAMM: Do you remember your father?
> CLOV (*wearily*): Same answer. (*Pause.*) You've asked me these
>   questions millions of times.
> HAMM: I love the old questions. (*With fervor.*) Ah the old
>   questions, the old answers, there's nothing like them.

Thoughts are dragged along and distorted like the day's leftovers, *homo homini sapienti sat.* Hence the precariousness of what Beckett refuses to deal with, interpretation. He shrugs his shoulders about the possibility of philosophy today, or theory in general. The irrationality of bourgeois society on the wane resists being understood: those were the good old days when a critique of political economy could be written which took this society by its own ratio. For in the meantime it has thrown this ratio on the junkheap and virtually replaced it with direct control. The interpretive word, therefore, cannot recuperate Beckett, while his dramaturgy—precisely by virtue of its limitation to exploded facticity—twitches beyond it, pointing toward interpretation in its essence as riddle. One could almost designate as the criterion of relevant philosophy today whether it is up to that task.

French existentialism had tackled history. In Beckett, history devours existentialism. In *Endgame,* a historical moment is revealed, the experience which was cited in the title of the culture industry's rubbish book *Corpsed.* After the Second War, everything is destroyed, even resurrected culture, without knowing it; humanity vegetates along, crawling, after events which even the survivors cannot really survive, on a pile of ruins which even renders futile self-reflection of one's own battered state. From the marketplace, as the play's pragmatic precondition, that fact is ripped away:

> CLOV: (*He gets up on ladder, turns the telescope on the without.*)
> Let's see. (*He looks, moving the telescope.*) Zero . . . (*he looks*) . . . zero . . . (*he looks*) . . . and zero.
> HAMM: Nothing stirs. All is—
> CLOV: Zer—
> HAMM (*violently*): Wait till you're spoken to. (*Normal voice.*)
> All is . . . all is . . . all is what? (*Violently.*) All is what?
> CLOV: What all is? In a word. Is that what you want to know?
> Just a moment. (*He turns the telescope on the without, looks, lowers the telescope, turns toward Hamm.*) Corpsed. (*Pause.*)
> Well? Content?

That all human beings are dead is covertly smuggled in. An earlier passage explains why the catastrophe may not be mentioned. Vaguely, Hamm himself is to blame for that:

> HAMM: That old doctor, he's dead naturally?
> CLOV: He wasn't old.
> HAMM: But he's dead?
> CLOV: Naturally. (*Pause.*) *You* ask *me* that?

The condition presented in the play is nothing other than that in which "there's no more nature." Indistinguishable is the phase of completed reification of the world, which leaves no remainder of what was not made by humans; it is permanent catastrophe, along with a catastrophic event caused by humans themselves, in which nature has been extinguished and nothing grows any longer.

> HAMM: Did your seeds come up?
> CLOV: No.
> HAMM: Did you scratch round them to see if they had
>   sprouted?
> CLOV: They haven't sprouted.
> HAMM: Perhaps it's still too early.
> CLOV: If they were going to sprout they would have sprouted.
>   (*Violently.*) They'll never sprout!

The dramatis personae resemble those who dream their own death, in a "shelter" where "it's time it ended." The end of the world is discounted, as if it were a matter of course. Every supposed drama of the atomic age would mock itself, if only because its fable would hopelessly falsify the horror of historical anonymity by shoving it into the characters and actions of humans, and possibly by gaping at the "prominents" who decide whether the button will be pushed. The violence of the unspeakable is mimicked by the timidity to mention it. Beckett keeps it nebulous. One can only speak euphemistically about what is incommensurate with all experience, just as one speaks in Germany of the murder of the Jews. It has become a total a priori, so that bombed-out consciousness no longer has any position from which it could reflect on that fact. The desperate state of things supplies—with gruesome irony—a means of stylization that protects that pragmatic precondition from any contamination by childish science fiction. If Clov really were exaggerating, as his nagging, "common-sensical" companion reproaches him, that would not change much. If catastrophe amounted to a partial end of the world, that would be a bad joke: then nature, from which the imprisoned figures are cut off, would be as good as nonexistent; what remains of it would only prolong the torment.

This historical nota bene however, this parody of the Kierkegaardian one of the convergence of time and eternity, imposes at the same time a taboo on history. What would be called the *condition humaine* in existentialist jargon is the image of the last human, which is devouring the earlier ones—humanity. Existential ontology asserts the universally valid in a process of abstraction which is not conscious of itself. While it still—according to the old phenomenological doctrine of the intuition of essence—behaves as if it were aware, even in the particular, of its binding determinations, thereby unifying apriority and concreteness, it nonetheless distills out what appears to transcend temporality. It does so by blotting out particularity—what is individualized in space and time, what makes existence existence rather than its mere concept. Ontology appeals to those who are weary of philosophical formalism but who yet cling to what is only accessible formally. To such unacknowledged abstraction, Beckett affixes the caustic antithesis by means of acknowledged subtraction. He does not leave out the temporality of existence—all existence, after all, is temporal—but rather removes from existence what time, the historical tendency, attempts to quash in reality. He lengthens the escape route of the subject's liquidation to the point where it constricts into a "this-here," whose abstractness—the loss of all qualities—extends ontological abstraction literally *ad absurdum*, to that Absurd which mere existence becomes as soon as it is consumed in naked self-identity. Childish foolishness emerges as the content of philosophy, which degenerates to tautology—to a conceptual duplication of that existence it had intended to comprehend. While recent ontology subsists on the unfulfilled promise of concretion of its abstractions, concreteness in Beckett—that shell-like, self-enclosed existence which is no longer capable of universality—but rather exhausts itself in pure self-positing—is obviously the same as an abstractness which is no longer capable of experience. Ontology arrives home as the pathogenesis of false life. It is depicted as the state of negative eternity. If the messianic Myshkin once forgot his watch because earthly time is invalid for him, then time is lost to his antipodes because it could still imply hope. The yawn accompanying the bored remark that the weather is "as usual" gapes like a hellish abyss:

> HAMM: But that's always the way at the end of the day, isn't it, Clov?
> CLOV: Always.
> HAMM: It's the end of the day like any other day, isn't it, Clov?
> CLOV: Looks like it.

Like time, the temporal itself is damaged; saying that it no longer exists would already be too comforting. It is and it is not, like the world for the solipsist who doubts its existence, while he must concede it with every sentence. Thus a passage of dialogue hovers:

> HAMM: And the horizon? Nothing on the horizon?
> CLOV (*lowering the telescope, turning towards Hamm, exasperated*):

What in God's name would there be on the horizon?
(*Pause.*)
HAMM: The waves, how are the waves?
CLOV: The waves? (*He turns the telescope on the waves.*) Lead.
HAMM: And the sun?
CLOV (*looking*): Zero.
HAMM: But it should be sinking. Look again.
CLOV (*looking*): Damn the sun.
HAMM: Is it night already then?
CLOV (*looking*): No.
HAMM: Then what is it?
CLOV (*looking*): Gray. (*Lowering the telescope, turning towards Hamm, louder.*) Gray! (*Pause. Still louder.*) GRRAY!

History is excluded, because it itself has dehydrated the power of consciousness to think history, the power of remembrance. Drama falls silent and becomes gesture, frozen amid the dialogues. Only the result of history appears—as decline. What preens itself in the existentialists as the once-and-for-all of being has withered to the sharp point of history which breaks off. [Georg] Lukács's objection, that in Beckett humans are reduced to animality (*The Meaning of Contemporary Realism,* trans. John and Necke Mander), resists with official optimism the fact that residual philosophies, which would like to bank the true and immutable after removing temporal contingency, have become the residue of life, the end product of injury. Admittedly, as nonsensical as it is to attribute to Beckett—as Lukács does— an abstract, subjectivist ontology and then to place it on the excavated index of degenerate art because of its worldlessness and infantility, it would be equally ridiculous to have him testify as a key political witness. For urging the struggle against atomic death, a work that notes that death's potential even in ancient struggles is hardly appropriate. The simplifier of terror refuses—unlike Brecht—any simplification. But he is not so dissimilar from Brecht, insofar as his differentiation becomes sensitivity to subjective differences, which have regressed to the "conspicuous consumption" of those who can afford individuation.

Therein lies social truth. Differentiation cannot absolutely or automatically be recorded as positive. The simplification of the social process now beginning relegates it to "incidental expenses" (*faux frais*), somewhat as the formalities of social forms, from which emerged the capability for differentiation, are disappearing. Differentiation, once the condition of humanity, glides into ideology. But the nonsentimental consciousness of that fact does not regress itself. In the act of omission, that which is omitted survives through its exclusion, as consonance survives in atonal harmony. The idiocy of *Endgame* is recorded and developed with the greatest differentiation. The unprotesting depiction of omnipresent regression protests against a disposition of the world which obeys the law of regression so obligingly, that a counternotion can no longer be conceived to be held against it. That it is only thus and not otherwise is carefully shown; a finely-tuned alarm system reports what belongs to the topology of the play and what does not. Delicately, Beckett suppresses the delicate elements no less than the brutal ones. The vanity of the individual who indicts society, while his rights themselves merge in the accumulation of the injustice of all individuals—disaster itself—is manifest in embarrassing declamations like the "Germany" poem of Karl Wolfskehl. The "too-late," the missed moment condemns such bombastic rhetoric to phraseology. Nothing of that sort in Beckett. Even the view that he negatively presents the negativity of the age would fit into a certain kind of conception, according to which people in the eastern satellite countries—where the revolution is carried out by bureaucratic degree—need only devote themselves happily to reflecting a happy-go-lucky age. Playing with elements of reality—devoid of any mirror-like reflection—, refusing to take a "position," and finding joy in such freedom as is prescribed: all of this reveals more than would be possible if a "revealer" were partisan. The name of disaster can only be spoken silently. Only in the terror of recent events is the terror of the whole ignited, but only there, not in gazing upon "origins." Humankind, whose general species-name fits badly into Beckett's linguistic landscape, is only that which humanity has become. As in utopia, the last days pass judgment on the species. But this lamentation—within mind itself—must reflect that lamenting has become impossible. No amount of weeping melts the armor; only that face remains on which the tears have dried up. That is the basis of a kind of artistic behavior denounced as inhuman by those whose humanity has already become an advertisement for inhumanity, even if they have as yet no notion of that fact. Among the motives for Beckett's regression to animal-like man, that is probably the deepest. By hiding its countenance, his poetic work participates in the absurd.

The catastrophes that inspire *Endgame* have exploded the individual whose substantiality and absoluteness was the common element between Kierkegaard, Jaspers, and the Sartrian version of existentialism. Even to the concentration camp victims, existentialism had attributed the freedom either inwardly to accept or reject the inflicted martyrdom. *Endgame* destroys such illusions. The individual as a historical category, as the result of the capitalist process of alienation and as a defiant protest against it, has itself become openly transitory. The individualist position belonged, as polar opposite, to the ontological tendency of every existentialism, even that of *Being and Time*. Beckett's dramaturgy abandons it like an obsolete bunker. In its narrowness and contingency, individual experience could nowhere locate the authority to interpret itself as a cipher of being, unless it pronounced itself the fundamental characteristic of being. Precisely that, however, is untrue. The immediacy of individuation was deceptive: what particular human experience clings to is mediated, determined. *Endgame* insinuates that the individual's claim of autonomy and of being has become incredible. But while the prison of individuation is revealed as a prison and simultaneously as mere semblance—the stage scenery is the image of such self-reflection—, art is unable to release the spell of fragmented subjectivity; it can only depict solipsism. Beckett thereby bumps up against art's contemporary antinomy. The position of the absolute subject, once it has been cracked open as the appearance of an over-arching whole through which it first matures, cannot be maintained: Expressionism becomes obsolete. Yet the transition to the binding universality of objective reality, that universality which could relativize the semblance of individuation, is denied art. For art is different from the discursive cognition of the real, not gradually but categorically distinct from it; in art, only what is transported into the realm of subjectivity, commensurable to it, is valid. It can conceive reconciliation—its idea—only as reconciliation of that which is alienated. If art simulated the state of reconciliation by surrendering to the mere world of things, then it would negate itself. What is offered in the way of socialist realism is not—as some claim—beyond subjectivism but rather lags behind it and is at the same time its preartistic complement; the expressionist "Oh Man" and ideologically spiced social reportage fit together seamlessly. In art, unreconciled reality tolerates no reconciliation with the object; realism, which does not reach the level of subjective experience, to say nothing of reaching further, merely mimics reconciliation. The dignity of art today is not measured by asking whether it slips out of this antinomy by luck or cleverness, but whether art confronts and develops it. In that regard, *Endgame* is exemplary. It yields both to the impossibility of dealing with materials and of representation according to nineteenth-century practice, as well as to the insight that subjective modes of reaction, which mediate the laws of form rather than reflecting reality, are themselves no absolute first principle but rather a last principle, objectively posited. All content of subjectivity, which necessarily hypostatizes itself, is trace and shadow of the world, from which it withdraws in order not to serve that semblance

and conformity the world demands. Beckett responds to that condition not
with any immutable "provisions" (*Vorrat*), but rather with what is still
permitted, precariously and uncertainly, by the antagonistic tendencies. His
dramaturgy resembles the fun that the old Germany offered—knocking
about between the border markers of Baden and Bavaria, as if they fenced
in a realm of freedom. *Endgame* takes place in a zone of indifference between
inner and outer, neutral between—on the one hand—the "materials" without which subjectivity could not manifest itself or even exist, and—on the
other—an animating impulse which blurs the materials, as if that impulse
had breathed on the glass through which they are viewed. These materials
are so meager that aesthetic formalism is ironically rescued—against its
adversaries hither and thither, the stuff-pushers of dialectical materialism
and the administrators of authentic messages. The concreteness of the le-
murs, whose horizon was lost in a double sense, is transformed directly
into the most extreme abstraction; the level of material itself determines a
procedure in which the materials, by being lightly touched as transitory,
approximate geometrical forms; the most narrow becomes the general. The
localization of *Endgame* in that zone teases the spectator with the suggestion
of a symbolism which it—like Kafka—refuses. Because no state of affairs
is merely what it is, each appears as the sign of interiority, but that inward
element supposedly signified no longer exists, and the signs mean just that.
The iron ration of reality and people, with whom the drama reckons and
keeps house, is one with that which remains of subject, mind (*Geist*), and
soul in the face of permanent catastrophe: of the mind, which originated
in mimesis, only ridiculous imitation; of the soul—staging itself—inhumane
sentimentality; of the subject its most abstract determination, actually existing and thereby already blaspheming. Beckett's figures behave primi-
tively and behavioristically, corresponding to conditions after the
catastrophe, which has mutilated them to such an extent that they cannot
react differently—flies that twitch after the swatter has half smashed them.
The aesthetic *principium stilisationis* does the same to humans. Thrown back
completely upon themselves, subjects—anticosmism become flesh—consist
in nothing other than the wretched realities of their world, shrivelled down
to raw necessities; they are empty personae, through which the world truly
can only resound. Their "phonyness" is the result of mind's disenchant-
ment—as mythology. In order to undercut history and perhaps thereby to
hibernate, *Endgame* occupies the nadir of what philosophy's construction
of the subject-object confiscated at its zenith: pure identity becomes the
identity of annihilation, identity of subject and object in the state of complete
alienation. While meanings in Kafka were beheaded or confused, Beckett

calls a halt to the bad infinity of intentions: their sense is senselessness. Objectively and without any polemical intent, that is his answer to existential philosophy, which under the name of "thrownness" and later of "absurdity" transforms senselessness itself into sense, exploiting the equivocations inherent in the concept of sense. To this Beckett juxtaposes no world view, rather he takes it at its word. What becomes of the absurd, after the characters of the meaning of existence have been torn down, is no longer a universal—the absurd would then be yet again an idea—but only pathetic details which ridicule conceptuality, a stratum of utensils as in an emergency refuge: ice boxes, lameness, blindness, and unappetizing bodily functions. Everything awaits evacuation. This stratum is not symbolic but rather the postpsychological state, as in old people and torture victims.

Removed from their inwardness, Heidegger's states of being (*Befindlichkeiten*) and Jaspers's "situations" have become materialistic. With them, the hypostatis of individual and that of situation were in harmony. The "situation" was temporal existence itself, and the totality of living individuals was the primary certainty. It presupposed personal identity: Here, Beckett proves to be a pupil of Proust and a friend of Joyce, in that he gives back to the concept of "situation" what it actually says and what philosophy made vanish by exploiting it: dissociation of the unity of consciousness into disparate elements—nonidentity. As soon as the subject is no longer doubtlessly self-identical, no longer a closed structure of meaning, the line of demarcation with the exterior becomes blurred, and the situations of inwardness become at the same time physical ones. The tribunal over individuality—conserved by existentialism as its idealist core—condemns idealism. Nonidentity is both: the historical disintegration of the subject's unity and the emergence of what is not itself subject. That changes the possible meaning of "situation." It is defined by Jaspers as "a reality for an existing subject who has a stake in it" (*Philosophy,* trans. E. B. Ashton). He subsumes the concept of situation under a subject conceived as firm and identical, just as he insinuates that meaning accrues to the situation because of its relationship to this subject. Immediately thereafter, he also calls it "not just a reality governed by natural laws. It is a sense-related reality," a reality moreover which, strangely enough, is said by Jaspers to be "neither psychological nor physical, but both in one." When situation becomes— in Beckett's view—actually both, it loses its existential-ontological constituents: personal identity and meaning. That becomes striking in the concept of "boundary situation" (*Grenzsituation*). It also stems from Jaspers: "Situations like the following: that I am always in situations; that I cannot live without struggling and suffering; that I cannot avoid guilt; that I must die—these are what I call boundary situations. They never change, except in appearance; [with regard to our existence, they are final]." The construction of *Endgame* takes that up with a sardonic "Pardon me?" Such wise sayings as that "I cannot live without suffering, that I cannot avoid guilt, that I must die" lose their triviality the moment they are retrieved back from their apriority and portrayed concretely. Then they break to pieces— all those noble, affirmative elements with which philosophy adorns that existence that Hegel already called "foul" (*faul*). It does so by subsuming the nonconceptual under a concept, which magically disperses that difference pompously characterized as "ontological." Beckett turns existential philosophy from its head back on its feet. His play reacts to the comical and ideological mischief of sentences like: "Courage in the boundary situation is an attitude that lets me view death as an indefinite opportunity to be myself," whether Beckett is familiar with them or not. The misery of participants in the *Endgame* is the misery of philosophy.

These Beckettian situations which constitute his drama are the negative of meaningful reality. Their models are those of empirical reality. As soon as they are isolated and divested of their purposeful and psychological context through the loss of personal unity, they assume a specific and compelling expression—that of horror. They are manifest already in the practice of Expressionism. The dread disseminated by Leonhard Frank's elementary school teacher Mager, the cause of his murder, becomes evident in the description of Mager's fussy manner of peeling an apple in class. Although it seems so innocent, such circumspection is the figure of sadism: this image of one who takes his time resembles that of the one who delays giving a ghastly punishment. Beckett's treatment of these situations, that panicky and yet artificial derivation of simplistic slapstick comedy of yesteryear, articulates a content noted already in Proust. In his posthumous work *Immediacy and Sense-Interpretation*, Heinrich Rickert considers the possibility of an objective physiognomy of mind, rather than of a merely projected "soul" of a landscape or a work of art. He cites a passage from Ernst Robert Curtius, who considers it "only partially correct to view Proust only or primarily as a great psychologist. A Stendhal is appropriately characterized in this manner. He is indeed part of the Cartesian tradition of the French mind. But Proust does not recognize the division between thinking and the extended substance. He does not sever the world into psychological and physical parts. To regard his work from the perspective of the 'psychological novel' is to misunderstand its significance. In Proust's books, the world of sensate objects occupies the same space as that of mind." Or: "If Proust is a psychologist, he is one in a completely new sense—by immersing all reality, including sense perception, in a mental fluid." To show "that the usual concept of the psychic is not appropriate here," Rickert again quotes Curtius: "But here the concept of the psychological has lost its opposite—and is thereby no longer a useful characterization." The physiognomy of objective expression however retains an enigma. The situations say something, but what? In this regard, art itself, as the embodiment of situations, converges with that physiognomy. It combines the most extreme determinacy with its radical opposite. In Beckett, this contradiction is inverted outward. What is otherwise entrenched behind a communicative facade is here condemned merely to appear. Proust, in a subterranean mystical tradition, still clings affirmatively to that physiognomy, as if involuntary memory disclosed a secret language of things; in Beckett, it becomes the physiognomy of what is no longer human. His situations are counterparts to the immutable elements conjured by Proust's situations; they are wrested from the flood of schizophrenia, which fearful "health" resists with murderous cries. In this realm Beckett's drama remains master of itself, transforming even schizophrenia into reflection:

> HAMM: I once knew a madman who thought the end of the
> world had come. He was a painter—and engraver. I had a
> great fondness for him. I used to go and see him, in the
> asylum. I'd take him by the hand and drag him to the
> window. Look! There! All that rising corn! And there!
> Look! The sails of the herring fleet! All that loveliness!
> (*Pause.*) He'd snatch away his hand and go back into his
> corner. Appalled. All he had seen was ashes. (*Pause.*) He
> alone had been spared. (*Pause.*) Forgotten. (*Pause.*) It
> appears the case is . . . was not so . . . so unusual.

The madman's perception would approximate that of Clov peering on command through the window. *Endgame* draws back from the nadir through no other means than by calling to itself like a sleepwalker: negation of negativity. There sticks in Beckett's memory something like an apoplectic middle-aged man taking his midday nap, with a cloth over his eyes to keep out the light or the flies; it makes him unrecognizable. This image—average and optically barely unusual—becomes a sign only for that gaze which perceives the face's loss of identity, sees the possibility that being concealed is the face of a dead man, and becomes aware of the repulsive nature of that physical concern which reduces the man to his body and places him already among corpses. Beckett stares at such aspects until that family routine—from which they stem—pales into irrelevance. The tableau begins with Hamm covered by an old sheet; at the end, he places near his face the handkerchief, his last possession:

> HAMM: Old Stancher! (*Pause.*) You . . . remain.

Such situations, emancipated from their context and from personal character, are reconstructed in a second autonomous context, just as music joins together the intentions and states of expression immersed in it until its sequence becomes a structure in its own right. A key point in the drama—"If I can hold my peace, and sit quiet, it will be all over with sound, and motion, all over and done with"—betrays the principle, perhaps as a reminiscence of how Shakespeare employed his principle in the actors' scene of *Hamlet*.

> HAMM: Then babble, babble, words, like the solitary child
> who turns himself into children, two, three, so as to be
> together, and whisper together, in the dark. (*Pause.*)
> Moment upon moment, pattering down, like the millet
> grains of . . . (*he hesitates*) that old Greek, and all life long
> you wait for that to mount up to a life.

In the tremors of "not being in a hurry," such situations allude to the indifference and superfluity of what the subject can still manage to do. While Hamm considers riveting shut the lids of those trash cans where his parents reside, he retracts that decision with the same words as when he must urinate with the tortuous aid of the catheter: "Time enough." The imperceptible aversion to medicine bottles, dating back to the moment one perceived one's parents as physically vulnerable, mortal, deteriorating, reappears in the question:

> HAMM: Is it not time for my pain-killer?

Speaking to each other has completely become Strindbergian grumbling:

> HAMM: You feel normal?
> CLOV (*irritably*): I tell you I don't complain.

And another time:

> HAMM: I feel a little too far to the left. (*Clov moves chair
> slightly.*) Now I feel a little too far to the right. (*Clov
> moves chair slightly.*) Now I feel a little too far forward.
> (*Clov moves chair slightly.*) Now I feel a little too far back.
> (*Clov moves chair slightly.*) Don't stay there, (*i.e. behind the
> chair*) you give me the shivers. (*Clov returns to his place
> beside the chair.*)
> CLOV: If I could kill him I'd die happy.

The waning of a marriage is the situation where one scratches the other:

> NELL: I am going to leave you.
> NAGG: Could you give me a scratch before you go?
> NELL: No. (*Pause.*) Where?
> NAGG: In the back.
> NELL: No. (*Pause.*) Rub yourself against the rim.
> NAGG: It's lower down. In the hollow.
> NELL: What hollow?
> NAGG: The hollow! (*Pause.*) Could you not? (*Pause.*) Yesterday
> you scratched me there.
> NELL (*elegiac*): Ah yesterday!
> NAGG: Could you not? (*Pause.*) Would you like me to scratch
> you? (*Pause.*) Are you crying again?
> NELL: I was trying.

After the dismissed father—preceptor of his parents—has told the Jewish joke, metaphysically famous, about the trousers and the world, he himself bursts into laughter. The shame which grips the listener when someone laughs at his own words becomes existential; life is merely the epitome of everything about which one must be ashamed. Subjectivity is frightening when it simply amounts to domination, as in the situation where one whistles and the other comes running. But what shame struggles against has its social function: in those moments when the bourgeois (*Bürger*) acts like a real bourgeois, he besmirches the concept of humanity on which his claim rests. Beckett's archaic images (*Urbilder*) are also historical, in that he shows as humanly typical only those deformations inflicted on humans by the form of their society. No space remains for anything else. The rudeness and ticks of normal character, which *Endgame* inconceivably intensifies, is that universality of the whole that already preforms all classes and individuals; it merely reproduces itself through bad particularity, the antagonistic interests of single individuals. Because there was no other life than the false one, the catalogue of its defects becomes the mirror image of ontology.

This shattering into unconnected, nonidentical elements is nevertheless tied to identity in a theater play, which does not abandon the traditional cast of characters. Only against identity, by dismantling its concept, is dissociation at all possible; otherwise, it would be pure, unpolemical, innocent pluralism. For the time being, the historical crisis of the individual runs up against the single biological being, its arena. The succession of situations in Beckett, gliding along without resistance from individuals, thus ends with those obstinate bodies to which they have regressed. Measured by a unit, such as the body, the schizoid situations are comical like optical illusions. That explains the *prima vista* clowning evident in the behavior and constellations of Beckett's figures. Psychoanalysis explains clownish humor as a regression back to a primordial ontogenetic level, and Beckett's regressive play descends to that level. But the laughter it inspires ought to suffocate the laughter. That is what happened to humor, after it became—as an aesthetic medium—obsolete, repulsive, devoid of any canon of what can be laughed at; without any place for reconciliation, where one could laugh; without anything between heaven and earth harmless enough to be laughed at. An intentionally idiotic double entendre about the weather runs:

> CLOV: Things are livening up. (*He gets up on the ladder, raises the telescope, lets it fall.*) It did it on purpose. (*He gets down, picks up the telescope, turns it on auditorium.*) I see . . . a multitude . . . in transports . . . of joy. (*Pause.*) That's what I call a magnifier. (*He lowers the telescope, turns toward Hamm.*) Well? Don't we laugh?

Humor itself has become foolish, ridiculous—who could still laugh at basic comic texts like *Don Quixote* or *Gargantua*—and Beckett carries out the verdict on humor. The jokes of the damaged people are themselves damaged. They no longer reach anybody; the state of decline, admittedly a part of all jokes, the *Kalauer*, now covers them like a rash. When Clov, looking through the telescope, is asked about the weather and frightens Hamm with the word "gray," he corrects himself with the formulation "a light black." That smears the punchline from Molière's *Miser*, who describes the allegedly stolen casket as gray-red. The marrow has been sucked out of the joke as well as out of the colors. At one point, the two antiheroes, a blind man and a lame man—the stronger is already both while the weaker will become so—come up with a "trick," an escape, "some kind of plan" à la *Three Penny Opera*; but they do not know whether it will only lengthen their lives and torment, or whether both are to end with absolute obliteration:

> CLOV: Ah good. (*He starts pacing to and fro, his eyes fixed on the ground, his hands behind his back. He halts.*) The pains in my legs! It's unbelievable! Soon I won't be able to think any more.
> HAMM: You won't be able to leave me. (*Clov resumes his pacing.*) What are you doing?
> CLOV: Having an idea. (*He paces.*) Ah. (*He halts.*)

HAMM: What a brain! (*Pause.*) Well?
CLOV: Wait! (*He meditates. Not very convinced.*) Yes . . . (*Pause. More convinced.*) Yes! (*He raises his head.*) I have it! I set the alarm!

That is probably associated with the originally Jewish joke from the Busch circus, when stupid August, who has caught his wife with his friend on the sofa, cannot decide whether to throw out his wife or the friend, because they are both so dear to him, and comes up with the idea of selling the sofa. But even the remaining trace of silly, sophistic rationality is wiped away. The only comical thing remaining is that along with the sense of the punchline, comedy itself has evaporated. That is how someone suddenly jerks upright after climbing to the top step, climbing further, and stepping into the void. The most extreme crudity completes the verdict on laughter, which has long since participated in its own guilt. Hamm lets his stumps of parents completely starve, those parents who have become babies in their trashcans—the son's triumph as a father. There is this chatter:

NAGG: Me pap!
HAMM: Accursed progenitor!
NAGG: Me pap!
HAMM: The old folks at home! No decency left! Guzzle,
    guzzle, that's all they think of. (*He whistles. Enter Clov.
    He halts beside the chair.*) Well! I thought you were leaving
    me.
CLOV: Oh not just yet, not just yet.
NAGG: Me pap!
HAMM: Give him his pap.
CLOV: There's no more pap.
HAMM (*to Nagg*): Do you hear that? There's no more pap.
    You'll never get any more pap.

To the irreparable harm already done, the antihero adds his scorn—the indignation at the old people who have no manners, just as the latter customarily decry dissolute youth. What remains humane in this scene—that the two old people share the zwieback with each other—becomes repulsive through its contrast with transcendental bestiality; the residue of love becomes the intimacy of smacking. As far as they are still human, they "humanize":

NELL: What is it, my pet? (*Pause.*) Time for love?
NAGG: Were you asleep?

NELL: Oh no!

NAGG: Kiss me.

NELL: We can't.

NAGG: Try. (*Their heads strain towards each other, fail to meet, fall apart again.*)

Dramatic categories as a whole are treated just like humor. All are parodied. But not ridiculed. Emphatically, parody entails the use of forms in the epoch of their impossibility. It demonstrates this impossibility and thereby changes the forms. The three Aristotelian unities are retained, but drama itself perishes. Along with subjectivity, whose final epilogue (*Nachspiel*) is *Endgame,* the hero is also withdrawn; the drama's freedom is only the impotent, pathetic reflex of futile resolutions. In that regard, too Beckett's drama is heir to Kafka's novels, to whom he stands in a similar relation as the serial composers to Schönberg: he reflects the precursor in himself, altering the latter through the totality of his principle. Beckett's critique of the earlier writer, which irrefutably stresses the divergence between what happens and the objectively pure, epic language, conceals the same difficulty as that confronted by contemporary integral composition with the antagonistic procedure of Schönberg. What is the raison d'être of forms when the tension between them and what is not homogeneous to them disappears, and when one nevertheless cannot halt the progress of mastery over aesthetic material? *Endgame* pulls out of the fray, by making that question its own, by making it thematic. That which prohibits the dramatization of Kafka's novels becomes subject matter. Dramatic components reappear after their demise. Exposition, complication, plot, peripeteia, and catastrophe return as decomposed elements in a post-mortem examination of dramaturgy: the news that there are no more painkillers depicts catastrophe. Those components have been toppled along with that meaning once discharged by drama; *Endgame* studies (as if in a test-tube) the drama of the age, the age that no longer tolerates what constitutes drama. For example, tragedy, at the height of its plot and with antithesis as its quintessence, manifested the utmost tightening of the dramatic thread, stychomythia—dialogues in which the trimeter spoken by one person follows that of the other. Drama had renounced this technique, because its stylization and resulting pretentiousness seemed alien to secular society. Beckett employs it as if the detonation had revealed what was buried in drama. *Endgame* contains rapid, monosyllabic dialogues, like the earlier question-and-answer games between the blinded king and fate's messenger. But where the bind tightened then, the speakers now grow slack. Short of breath until they almost fall silent, they no longer manage the synthesis of linguistic phrases; they stammer in protocol sentences that might stem from positivists or Expressionists. The boundary value (*Grenzwert*) of Beckett's drama is that silence already defined as "the rest" in Shakespeare's inauguration of modern tragedy. The fact that an "act without words" follows *Endgame* as a kind of epilogue is its own *terminus ad quem*. The words resound like merely makeshift ones because silence is not yet entirely successful, like voices accompanying and disturbing it.

What becomes of form in *Endgame* can be virtually reconstructed from literary history. In Ibsen's *The Wild Duck,* the degenerate photographer Hjalmar Ekdal—himself a potential antihero—forgets to bring to the teenager Hedwig the promised menu from the sumptuous dinner at old Werle's house, to which he had been invited without his family. Psychologically, that is motivated by his slovenly egotistical character, but it is symbolically significant also for Hjalmar, for the course of the plot, and for the play's meaning: the girl's futile sacrifice. That anticipates the later Freudian theory of "parapraxis," which explicates such slip-ups by means of their relation to past experiences and wishes of an individual, to the individual's identity. Freud's hypotheses, "all our experiences have a sense," transforms the traditional dramatic idea into psychological realism, from which Ibsen's tragi-comedy of the *Wild Duck* incomparably extracts the spark of form one more time. When such symbolism liberates itself from its psychological determination, it congeals into a being-in-itself, and the symbol becomes symbolic as in Ibsen's late works like *John Gabriel Borkmann,* where the accountant Foldal is overcome by so-called "youth." The contradiction between such a consistent symbolism and conservative realism constitutes the inadequacy of the late plays. But it thereby also constitutes the leavening ferment of the Expressionist Strindberg. His symbols, torn away from empirical human beings, are woven into a tapestry in which everything and nothing is symbolic, because everything can signify everything. Drama need only become aware of the ineluctably ridiculous nature of such pansymbolism, which destroys itself; it need only take that up and utilize it, and Beckettian absurdity is already achieved as a result of the immanent dialectic of form. Not meaning anything becomes the only meaning. The mortal fear of the dramatic figures, if not of the parodied drama itself, is the distortedly comical fear that they could mean something or other:

> HAMM: We're not beginning to . . . to . . . mean something?
> CLOV: Mean something! You and I, mean something! (*Brief laugh.*) Ah that's a good one!

With this possibility, long since crushed by the overwhelming power of an apparatus in which individuals are interchangeable and superfluous, the meaning of language also disappears. Hamm, irritated by the impulse of life which has regressed to clumsiness in his parents' trashcan conversations, and nervous because "it doesn't end," asks: "Will you never finish? Will this never finish?" The play takes place on that level. It is constructed on the ground of a proscription of language, and it articulates that in its own structure. However, it does not thereby avoid the aporia of Expressionist drama: that language, even where it tends to be shortened to mere sound, yet cannot shake off its semantic element. It cannot become purely mimetic or gestural, just as forms of modern painting, liberated from referentiality (*Gegenständlichkeit*), cannot cast off all similarity to objects. Mimetic values, definitively unloosed from significative ones, then approach arbitrariness, contingency, and finally a mere secondary convention. The way *Endgame* comes to terms with that differentiates it from *Finnegans Wake*. Rather than striving to liquidate the discursive element of language through pure sound, Beckett turns that element into an instrument of its own absurdity and he does that according to the ritual of clowns, whose babbling becomes nonsensical by presenting itself as sense. The objective disintegration of language—that simultaneously stereotyped and faulty chatter of self-alienation, where word and sentence melt together in human mouths—penetrates the aesthetic arcanum. The second language of those falling silent, a conglomeration of insolent phrases, pseudological connections, and galvanized words appearing as commodity signs—as the desolate echo of the advertising world—is "refunctioned" (*umfunktioniert*) into the language of a poetic work that negates language. Beckett thus approximates the drama of Eugène Ionesco. Whereas a later work by him is organized around the image of the tape recorder, the language of *Endgame* resembles another language familiar from the loathsome party game, where someone records the nonsense spoken at a party and then plays it back for the guests' humiliation. The shock, overcome on such an occasion only by stupid tittering, is here carefully composed. Just as alert experience seems to notice everywhere situations from Kafka's novels after reading him intensely, so does Beckett's language bring about a healing illness of those already ill: whoever listens to himself worries that he also talks like that. For some time now, the accidental events on the street seem to the moviegoer just leaving the theater like the planned contingency of a film. Between the mechanically assembled phrases taken from the language of daily life, the chasm yawns. Where one of the pair asks with the routine gesture of the hardened man, certain of the uncontestable boredom of existence, "What in God's name could there be on the horizon?" then this shoulder-shrugging in language becomes apocalyptic, particularly because it is so familiar. From the bland yet aggressive impulse of human "common sense," "What do you think there is?" is extracted the confession of its own nihilism. Somewhat later, Hamm the master commands the *soi-disant* servant Clov, in a circus-task, to undertake the vain attempt to shove the chair back and forth, to fetch the "gaff." There follows a brief dialogue:

> CLOV: Do this, do that, and I do it. I never refuse. Why?
> HAMM: You're not able to.
> CLOV: Soon I won't do it any more.
> HAMM: You won't be able to any more. (*Exit Clov.*) Ah the
> creatures, everything has to be explained to them.

That "everything has to be explained to the creatures" is drummed daily by millions of superiors into millions of subordinates. However, by means of the nonsense thus supposedly established in the passage—Hamm's explanation contradicts his own command—the cliché's inanity, usually hidden by custom, is garishly illuminated, and furthermore, the fraud of speaking with each other is expressed. When conversing, people remain hopelessly distant from each other no more reaching each other than the two old cripples in the trash bins do. Communication, the universal law of clichés, proclaims that there is no more communication. The absurdity of all speaking is not unrelated to realism but rather develops from it. For communicative language postulates—already in its syntactic form, through logic, the nature of conclusions, and stable concepts—the principle of sufficient reason. Yet this requirement is hardly met any more: when people speak with each other, they are motivated partly by their psychology or prelogical unconscious, and partly by their pursuit of purposes. Since they aim at self-preservation, these purposes deviate from that objectivity deceptively manifest in their logical form. At any rate, one can prove that point to people today with the help of tape recorders. In Freud's as in Pareto's understanding, the ratio of verbal communication is always also a rationalization. *Ratio* itself emerged from the interest in self-preservation, and it is therefore undermined by the obligatory rationalizations of its own irrationality. The contradiction between the rational facade and the immutably irrational is itself already the absurd. Beckett must only mark the contradiction and employ it as a selective principle, and realism, casting off the illusion of rational stringency, comes into its own.

Even the syntactic form of question and answer is undermined. It presupposes an openness of what is to be spoken, an openness which no

longer exists, as Huxley already noted. In the question one hears already
the anticipated answer, and that condemns the game of question and answer
to empty deception, to the unworkable effort to conceal the unfreedom of
informative language in the linguistic gesture of freedom. Beckett tears
away this veil, and the philosophical veil as well. Everything radically called
into question when confronted by nothingness resists—by virtue of a pathos
borrowed from theology—these terrifying consequences, while insisting
on their possibility; in the form of question and answer, the answer is
infiltrated with the meaning denied by the whole game. It is not for nothing
that in fascism and prefascism such destructionists were able heartily to
scorn destructive intellect. But Beckett deciphers the lie of the question
mark: the question has become rhetorical. While the existential-philosoph-
ical hell resembles a tunnel, where in the middle one can already discern
light shining at the end, Beckett's dialogues rip up the railroad tracks of
conservation; the train no longer arrives at the bright end of the tunnel.
Wedekind's old technique of misunderstanding becomes total. The course
of the dialogues themselves approximates the contingency principle of literary production. It sounds as if the laws of its continuation were not the
"reason" of speech and reply, and not even their psychological entwine-
ment, but rather a test of listening, related to that of a music which frees
itself from preformed types. The drama attends carefully to what kind of
sentence might follow another. Given the accessible spontaneity of such
questions, the absurdity of content is all the more strongly felt. That, too,
finds its infantile model in those people who, when visiting the zoo, wait
attentively for the next move of the hippopotamus or the chimpanzee.

In the state of its disintegration, language is polarized. On the one
hand, it becomes basic English, or French, or German—single words,
archaically ejected commands in the jargon of universal disregard, the intimacy of irreconcilable adversaries; on the other hand, it becomes the
aggregate of its empty forms, of a grammar that has renounced all reference
to its content and therefore also to its synthetic function. The interjections
are accompanied by exercise sentences, God knows why. Beckett trumpets
this from the rooftops, too: one of the rules of the *Endgame* is that the
unsocial partners—and with them the audience—are always eyeing each
other's cards. Hamm considers himself an artist. He has chosen as his life
maxim Nero's *qualis artifex pereo*. But the stories he undertakes run aground
on syntax:

> HAMM: Where was I? (*Pause. Gloomily.*) It's finished, we're
> finished. (*Pause.*) Nearly finished.

Logic reels between the linguistic paradigms. Hamm and Clov converse in their authoritative, mutually cutting fashion:

> HAMM: Open the window.
> CLOV: What for?
> HAMM: I want to hear the sea.
> CLOV: You wouldn't hear it.
> HAMM: Even if you opened the window?
> CLOV: No.
> HAMM: Then it's not worthwhile opening it?
> CLOV: No.
> HAMM (*violently*): Then open it! (*Clov gets up on the ladder, opens the window. Pause.*) Have you opened it?
> CLOV: Yes.

One could almost see in Hamm's last "then" the key to the play. Because it is not worthwhile to open the window, since Hamm cannot hear the sea—perhaps it is dried out, perhaps it no longer moves—he insists that Clov open it. The nonsense of an act becomes a reason to accomplish it— a late legitimation of Fichte's free activity for its own sake. That is how contemporary actions look, and they arouse the suspicion that things were never very different. The logical figure of the absurd, which makes the claim of stringency for stringency's contradictory opposite, denies every context of meaning apparently guaranteed by logic, in order to prove logic's own absurdity: that logic, by means of subject, predicate, and copula, treats nonidentity as if it were identical, as if it were consumed in its forms. The absurd does not take the place of the rational as one world view of another; in the absurd, the rational world view comes into its own.

The preestablished harmony of despair reigns between the forms and the residual content of the play. The ensemble—smelted together—counts only four heads. Two of them are excessively red, as if their vitality were a skin disease; the two old ones, however, are excessively white, like sprouting potatoes in a cellar. None of them still has a properly functioning body; the old people consist only of rumps, having apparently lost their legs not in the catastrophe but in a private tandem accident in the Ardennes, "on the road to Sedan," an area where one army regularly annihilates another. One should not suppose that all that much has changed. Even the memory of their own particular (*bestimmt*) misfortune becomes enviable in relation to the indeterminacy (*Unbestimmtheit*) or universal misfortune—they laugh at it. In contrast to Expressionism's fathers and sons, they all have their own names, but all four names have one syllable, "four-letter words" like

obscenities. Practical, familiar abbreviations, popular in Anglo-Saxon countries, are exposed as mere stumps of names. Only the name of the old
mother, Nell, is somewhat common even if obsolete; Dickens uses it for
the touching child in *Old Curiosity Shop*. The three other names are invented
as if for billboards. The old man is named Nagg, with the association of
"nagging" and perhaps also a German association: an intimate pair is intimate through "gnawing"(*Nagen*). They talk about whether the sawdust
in their cans has been changed; yet it is not sawdust but sand. Nagg stipulates
that it used to be sawdust, and Nell answers boredly: "Once!"—a woman
who spitefully exposes her husband's frozen, repetitive declarations. As
sordid as the fight about sawdust or sand is, the difference is decisive for
the residual plot, the transition from a minimum to nothing. Beckett can
claim for himself what Benjamin praised in Baudelaire, the ability to "express something extreme with extreme discretion;" the routine consolation
that things could be worse becomes a condemnation. In the realm between
life and death, where even pain is no longer possible, the difference between
sawdust and sand means everything. Sawdust, wretched by-product of the
world of things, is now in great demand; its removal becomes an inten-
sification of the lifelong death penalty. The fact that both lodge in trash
bins—a comparable motif appears, moreover, in Tennessee Williams's
Camino Real, surely without one play having been influenced by the other—
takes the conversational phrase literally, as in Kafka. "Today old people
are thrown in the trashcan" and it happens. *Endgame* is the true gerontology.
According to the measure of socially useful labor, which they can no longer
perform, old people are superfluous and must be discarded. That is extracted
from the scientific ruckus of a welfare system that accentuates what it
negates. *Endgame* trains the viewer for a condition where everyone involved
expects—upon lifting the lid from the nearest dumpster—to find his own
parents. The natural cohesion of life has become organic refuse. The national
socialists irreparably overturned the taboo of old age. Beckett's trashcans
are the emblem of a culture restored after Auschwitz. Yet the subplot goes
further than too far, to the old people's demise. They are denied children's
fare, their pap, which is replaced by a biscuit they—toothless—can no
longer chew; and they suffocate, because the last man is too sensitive to
grant life to the next-to-last ones. That is entwined with the main plot,
because the old pair's miserable end drives it forward to that exit of life
whose possibility constitutes the tension in the play. Hamlet is revised:
croak or croak, that is the question.

The name of Shakespeare's hero is grimly foreshortened by Beckett—
the last, liquidated dramatic subject echoing the first. It is also associated

with one of Noah's sons and thereby with the flood: the progenitor of blacks, who replaces the white "master race" in a Freudian negation. Finally, there is the English "ham actor." Beckett's Hamm, the key to power and helpless at the same time, plays at what he no longer is, as if he had read the most recent sociological literature defining *zoon politikon* as a role. Whoever cleverly presented himself became a "personality" just like helpless Hamm. "Personality" may have been a role originally—nature pretending to transcend nature. Fluctuation in the play's situations causes one of Hamm's roles: occasionally, a stage direction drastically suggests that he speak with the "voice of a rational being"; in a lengthy narrative, he is to strike a "narrative tone." The memory of what is irretrievably past becomes a swindle. Disintegration retrospectively condemns as fictional that continuity of life which alone made life possible. Differences in tone—between people who narrate and those who speak directly—pass judgment on the principle of identity. Both alternate in Hamm's long speech, a kind of inserted aria without music. At the transition points he pauses—the artistic pauses of the veteran actor of heroic roles. For the norm of existential philosophy—people should be themselves because they can no longer become anything else—*Endgame* posits the antithesis, that precisely this self is not a self but rather the aping imitation of something nonexistent. Hamm's mendacity exposes the lie concealed in saying "I" and thereby exhibiting substantiality, whose opposite is the content disclosed by the "I." Immutability, the epitome of transience, is its ideology. What used to be the truth content of the subject—thinking—is only still preserved in its gestural shell. Both main figures act as if they were reflecting on something, but without thinking.

> HAMM: The whole thing is comical, I grant you that. What
>   about having a good guffaw the two of us together?
> CLOV (*after reflection*): I couldn't guffaw today.
> HAMM (*after reflection*): Nor I.

According to his name, Hamm's counterpart is what he is, a truncated clown, whose last letter has been severed. An archaic expression for the devil sounds similar—cloven foot; it also resembles the current word "glove." He is the devil of his master, whom he has threatened with the worst, leaving him; yet at the same time he is also the glove with which the master touches the world of things, which he can no longer directly grasp. Not only the figure of Clov is constructed through such associations, but also his connection with the others. In the old piano edition of Stravinsky's "Ragtime for Eleven Instruments," one of the most significant works of his Surrealist phase, there was a Picasso drawing which—probably inspired by the title "rag"—showed two ragged figures, the ancestors of those vagabonds Vladimir and Estragon, who are waiting for Godot. This virtuoso sketch is a single entangled line. The double-sketch of *Endgame* is of this spirit, as well as the damaged repetitions irresistibly produced by Beckett's entire work. In them, history is cancelled out. This compulsory repetition is taken from the regressive behavior of someone locked up, who tries it again and again. Beckett converges with the newest musical tendencies by combining, as a Westerner, aspects of Stravinsky's radical past—the oppressive stasis of disintegrating continuity—with the most advanced expressive and constructive means from the Schönberg school. Even the outlines of Hamm and Clov are one line; they are denied the individuation of a tidily independent monad. They cannot live without each other. Hamm's power over Clov seems to be that only he knows how to open the cupboard, somewhat like the situation where only the principal knows the combination of the safe. He would reveal the secret to Clov, if Clov would swear to "finish" him—or "us." In a reply thoroughly characteristic of the play's tapestry, Clov answers: "I couldn't finish you"; as if the play were mocking the man who feigns reason, Hamm says: "Then you won't finish me." He is dependent on Clov, because Clov alone can accomplish what keeps both alive. But that is of questionable value, because both— like the captain of the ghostly ship—must fear not being able to die. The tiny bit that is also everything—that would be the possibility that something could perhaps change. This movement, or its absence, is the plot. Admittedly, it does not become much more explicit than the repeated motif "Something is taking its course," as abstract as the pure form of time. The Hegelian dialectic of master and slave, mentioned by Günther Anders with reference to *Godot,* is derided rather than portrayed according to the tenets of traditional aesthetics. The slave can no longer grasp the reins and abolish domination. Crippled as he is, he would hardly be capable of this, and according to the play's historico-philosophical sundial, it is too late for spontaneous action anyway. Clov has no other choice than to emigrate out into the world that no longer exists for the play's recluses, with a good chance of dying. He cannot even depend on freedom unto death. He does manage to make the decision to go, even comes in for the farewell: "Panama hat, tweed coat, raincoat over his arm, umbrella, bag"—a strong, almost musical conclusion. But one does not see his exit, rather he remains "impassive and motionless, his eyes fixed on Hamm, till the end." That is an allegory whose intention has evaporated. Aside from some differences, which may be decisive or completely irrelevant, this is identical with the beginning. No spectator and no philosopher can say if the play will not begin anew. The dialectic swings to a standstill.

As a whole, the play's plot is musically composed with two themes, like the double fugue of earlier times. The first theme is that it should end, a Schopenhauerian negation of the will to live become insignificant. Hamm strikes it up; the persons, no longer persons, become instruments of their situation, as if they were playing chamber music. "Of all of Beckett's bizarre instruments, Hamm, who in *Endgame* sits blindly and immovably in his wheelchair, resounds with the most tones, the most surprising sound." Hamm's nonidentity with himself motivates the course of the play. While he desires the end of the torment of a miserably infinite existence, he is concerned about his life, like a gentleman in his ominous "prime" years. The peripheral paraphernalia of health are utmost in his mind. Yet he does not fear death, rather that death could miscarry; Kafka's motif of the hunter Gracchus still resonates. Just as important to him as his own bodily necessities is the certainty that Clov, ordered to gaze out, does not espy any sail or trail of smoke, that no rat or insect is stirring, with whom the calamity could begin anew; that he also does not see the perhaps surviving child, who could signify hope and for whom he lies in wait like Herod the butcher for the *agnus dei*. Insecticide, which all along pointed toward the genocidal camps, becomes the final product of the domination of nature, which destroys itself. Only this content of life remains: that nothing be living. All existence is levelled to a life that is itself death, abstract domination. The second theme is attributed to Clov the servant. After an admittedly obscure history he sought refuge with Hamm; but he also resembles the son of the raging yet impotent patriarch. To give up obedience to the powerless is most difficult; the insignificant and obsolete struggles irresistibly against its abolition. Both plots are counterpointed, since Hamm's will to die is identical with his life principle, while Clov's will to live may well bring about the death of both; Hamm says: "Outside of here it's death." The antithesis of the heroes is also not fixed, rather their impulses converge; it is Clov who first speaks of the end. The scheme of the play's progression is the end game in chess, a typical, rather standard situation, separated from the middle game and its combinations by a caesura; these are also missing in the play, where intrigue and "plot" are silently suspended. Only artistic mistakes or accidents, such as something growing somewhere, could cause unforeseen events, but not resourceful spirit. The field is almost empty, and what happened before can only be poorly construed from the positions of the few remaining figures. Hamm is the king, about whom everything turns and who can do nothing himself. The in-

congruity between chess as pastime and the excessive effort involved becomes on the stage an incongruity between athletic pretense and the
lightweight actions that are performed. Whether the game ends with stalemate or with perpetual check, or whether Clov wins, remains unclear, as
if clarity in that would already be too much meaning. Moreover, it is
probably not so important, because everything would come to an end in
stalemate as in checkmate. Otherwise, only the fleeting image of the child
breaks out of the circle, the most feeble reminder of Fortinbras or the child
king. It could even be Clov's own abandoned child. But the oblique light
falling from thence into the room is as weak as the helplessly helping arms
extending from the windows at the conclusion of Kafka's *Trial*.

The history of the subject's end becomes thematic in an intermezzo,
which can afford its symbolism, because it depicts the subject's own de-
crepitude and therefore that of its meaning. The hubris of idealism, the
inthroning of man as creator in the center of creation, has entrenched itself
in that "bare interior" like a tyrant in his last days. There man repeats with
a reduced, tiny imagination what man was once supposed to be; man repeats
what was taken from him by social strictures as well as by today's cos-
mology, which he cannot escape. Clov is his male nurse. Hamm has himself
shoved about by Clov into the middle of that *intérieur* which the world has
become but which is also the interior of his own subjectivity:

> HAMM: Take me for a little turn. (*Clov goes behind the chair and
> pushes it forward.*) Not too fast! (*Clov pushes chair.*) Right
> round the world! (*Clov pushes chair.*) Hug the walls, then
> back to the center again. (*Clov pushes chair.*) I was right in
> the center, wasn't I?

The loss of the center, parodied here because that center itself was a lie,
becomes the paltry object of carping and powerless pedantry:

> CLOV: We haven't done the round.
> HAMM: Back to my place. (*Clov pushes chair back to center.*) Is
> that my place?
> CLOV: I'll measure it.
> HAMM: More or less! More or less!
> CLOV (*moving chair slightly*): There!
> HAMM: I'm more or less in the center?
> CLOV: I'd say so.
> HAMM: You'd say so! Put me right in the center!
> CLOV: I'll go and get the tape.
> HAMM: Roughly! Roughly! (*Clov moves chair slightly.*) Band in
> the center!

What is paid back in this ludicrous ritual is nothing originally perpetrated by the subject. Subjectivity itself is guilty; that one even is. Original sin is heretically fused with creation. Being, trumpeted by existential philosophy as the meaning of being, becomes its antithesis. Panic fear of the reflex movements of living entities does not only drive untiringly toward the domination of nature: it also attaches itself to life as the ground of that calamity which life has become:

> HAMM: All those I might have helped. (*Pause.*) Helped!
> (*Pause.*) Saved. (*Pause.*) Saved! (*Pause.*) The place was
> crawling with them! (*Pause. Violently.*) Use your head,
> can't you, use your head, you're on earth, there's no cure
> for that!

From that he draws the conclusion: "The end is in the beginning and yet you go on." The autonomous moral law reverts antinomically from pure domination over nature into the duty to exterminate, which always lurked in the background:

> HAMM: More complications. (*Clov gets down.*) Not an
> underplot, I trust. (*Clov moves ladder nearer window gets up
> on it, turns telescope on the without.*)
> CLOV (*dismayed*): Looks like a small boy!
> HAMM (*sarcastic*): A small . . . boy!
> CLOV: I'll go and see. (*He gets down, drops the telescope, goes
> toward door, turns.*)
> HAMM: No! (*Clov halts.*)
> CLOV: No? A potential procreator?

Such a total conception of duty stems from idealism, which is judged by a question the handicapped rebel Clov poses to his handicapped master:

> CLOV: Any particular sector you fancy? Or merely the whole
> thing?

That sounds like a reminder of Benjamin's insight that an intuited cell of reality counterbalances the remainder of the whole world. Totality, a pure postulate of the subject, is nothing. No sentence sounds more absurd than this most reasonable of sentences, which bargains "the whole thing" down to "merely," to the phantom of an anthropocentrically dominated world. As reasonable as this most absurd observation is, it is nevertheless impossible to dispute the absurd aspects of Beckett's play just because they are confiscated by hurried apologetics and a desire for easy disposal. *Ratio*, having been fully instrumentalized, and therefore devoid of self-reflection and of reflection on what it has excluded, must seek that meaning it has itself extinguished. But in the condition that necessarily gave rise to this question, no answer is possible other than nothingness, which the form of the answer already is. The historical inevitability of this absurdity allows it to seem ontological; that is the veil of delusion produced by history itself. Beckett's drama rips through this veil. The immanent contradiction of the absurd, reason terminating in senselessness, emphatically reveals the possibility of a truth which can no longer even be thought; it undermines the absolute claim exercized by what merely is. Negative ontology is the negation of ontology: history alone has brought to maturity what was appropriated by the mythic power of timelessness. The historical fiber of situation and language in Beckett does not concretize—*more philosophico*—something unhistorical: precisely this procedure, typical of existential dramatists, is both foreign to art and philosophically obsolete. Beckett's once-and-for-all is rather infinite catastrophe; only "that the earth is extinguished, although I never saw it lit" justifies Clov's answer to Hamm's question: "Do you not think this has gone on long enough?" "Yes." Prehistory goes on, and the phantasm of infinity is only its curse. After Clov, commanded to look outside, reports to the totally lame man what he sees of earth, Hamm entrusts to him his secret:

> CLOV (*absorbed*): Mmm.
> HAMM: Do you know what it is?
> CLOV (*as before*): Mmm.
> HAMM: I was never there.

Earth was never yet tread upon; the subject is not yet a subject.

Determinate negation becomes dramaturgical through consistent reversal. Both social partners qualify their insight that there is no more nature with the bourgeois "You exaggerate." Prudence and circumspection are the tried-and-true means of sabotaging contemplation. They cause only melancholy reflection:

> CLOV (*sadly*): No one that ever lived ever thought so crooked
>   as we.

Where they draw nearest to the truth, they experience their consciousness—doubly comical—as false consciousness; thus a condition is mirrored that reflection no longer reaches. The entire play is woven with the technique of reversal. It transfigures the empirical world into that world desultorily named already by the late Strindberg and in expressionism. "The whole house stinks of corpses . . . The whole universe." Hamm, who then says "to hell with the universe," is just as much the descendant of Fichte, who disdains the world as nothing more than raw material and mere product, as he is the one without hope except for the cosmic night, which he implores with poetic quotes. Absolute, the world becomes a hell; there is nothing else. Beckett graphically stresses Hamm's sentence: "Beyond is the . . . OTHER hell." With a Brechtian commentary, he lets the distorted metaphysics of "the here and now" shine through:

> CLOV: Do you believe in the life to come?
> HAMM: Mine was always like that. (*Exit Clov.*) Got him that
>   time!

In his conception, Benjamin's notion of the "dialectic at a standstill" comes into its own:

> HAMM: It will be the end and there I'll be, wondering what
>   can have brought it on and wondering what can have (*he*
>   *hesitates*) . . . why it was so long coming. (*Pause.*) There
>   I'll be, in the old shelter, alone against the silence and
>   . . . (*he hesitates*) . . . the stillness. If I can hold my peace,
>   and sit quiet, it will be all over with sound and motion,
>   all over and done with.

That "stillness" is the order which Clov supposedly loves and which he defines as the purpose of his functions:

> CLOV: A world where all would be silent and still and each
>   thing in its last place, under the last dust.

To be sure, the Old Testament saying "You shall become dust (*Staub*) again" is translated here into "dirt" (*Dreck*). In the play, the substance of life, a life that is death, is the excretions. But the imageless image of death is one of indifference. In it, the distinction disappears: the distinction between absolute domination, the hell in which time is banished into space, in which nothing will change any more—and the messianic condition where everything would be in its proper place. The ultimate absurdity is that the repose of nothingness and that of reconciliation cannot be distinguished from each other. Hope creeps out of a world in which it is no more conserved than pap and pralines, and back where it came from, back into death. From it, the play derives its only consolation, a stoic one:

> CLOV: There are so many terrible things now.
> HAMM: No, no, there are not so many now.

Consciousness begins to look its own demise in the eye, as if it wanted to survive the demise, as these two want to survive the destruction of their world. Proust, about whom the young Beckett wrote an essay, is said to have attempted to keep protocol on his own struggle with death, in notes which were to be integrated into the description of Bergotte's death. *Endgame* carries out this intention like a mandate from a testament.

Life in the Box

Hugh Kenner

The stage is a place to wait. The place itself waits, when no one is in it. When the curtain rises on *Endgame,* sheets drape all visible objects as in a furniture warehouse. Clov's first act is to uncurtain the two high windows and inspect the universe; his second is to remove the sheets and fold them carefully over his arm, disclosing two ash cans and a figure in an armchair. This is so plainly a metaphor for waking up that we fancy the stage, with its high peepholes, to be the inside of an immense skull. It is also a ritual for starting the play; Yeats arranged such a ritual for *At the Hawk's Well,* and specified a black cloth and a symbolic song. It is finally a removal from symbolic storage of the objects that will be needed during the course of the performance. When the theater is empty it is sensible to keep them covered against dust. So we are reminded at the outset that what we are to witness is a dusty dramatic exhibition, repeated and repeatable. The necessary objects include three additional players (two of them in ash cans). Since none of them will move from his station we can think of them after the performance as being kept permanently on stage, and covered with their dust cloths again until tomorrow night.

The rising of the curtain disclosed these sheeted forms; the removal of the sheets disclosed the protagonist and his ash cans; the next stage is for the protagonist to uncover his own face, which he does with a yawn, culminating this three-phase strip tease with the revelation of a very red face and black glasses. His name, we gather from the program, is Hamm,

From *Samuel Beckett: A Critical Study.* © 1961, 1968 by Hugh Kenner. University of California Press, 1961.

a name for an actor. He is also Hamlet, bounded in a nutshell, fancying himself king of infinite space, but troubled by bad dreams; he is also "a toppled Prospero," remarking partway through the play, with judicious pedantry, "our revels now are ended"; he is also the Hammer to which Clov, Nagg and Nell (Fr. *clou,* Ger. *Nagel,* Eng. *nail*) stand in passive relationship; by extension, a chess player ("Me—[*he yawns*]—to play"); but also (since Clov must wheel him about) himself a chessman, probably the imperiled King.

Nagg and Nell in their dustbins appear to be pawns; Clov, with his arbitrarily restricted movements ("I can't sit") and his equestrian background ("And your rounds? Always on foot?" "Sometimes on horse") resembles the Knight, and his perfectly cubical kitchen ("ten feet by ten feet by ten feet, nice dimensions, nice proportions") resembles a square on the chessboard translated into three dimensions. He moves back and forth, into it and out of it, coming to the succor of Hamm and then retreating. At the endgame's end the pawns are forever immobile and Clov is poised for a last departure from the board, the status quo forever menaced by an expected piece glimpsed through the window, and King Hamm abandoned in check:

> Old endgame lost of old, play and lose and have done with losing. . . . Since that's the way we're playing it, let's play it that way . . . and speak no more about it . . . speak no more.

Even if we had not the information that the author of this work has been known to spend hours playing chess with himself (a game at which you always lose), we should have been alerted to his long-standing interest in its strategy by the eleventh chapter of *Murphy,* where Murphy's first move against Mr. Endon, the standard P—K$_4$, is described as "the primary cause of all [his] subsequent difficulties." (The same might be said of getting born, an equally conventional opening.) Chess has several peculiarities which lend themselves to the metaphors of this jagged play. It is a game of leverage, in which the significance of a move may be out of all proportion to the local disturbance it effects ("A flea! This is awful! What a day!"). It is a game of silences, in which new situations are appraised: hence Beckett's most frequent stage direction, *"Pause."* It is a game of steady attrition; by the time we reach the endgame the board is nearly bare, as bare as Hamm's world where there are no more bicycle wheels, sugarplums, painkillers, or coffins, let alone people. And it is a game which by the successive removal of screening pieces constantly extends the range of lethal forces, until at the endgame peril from a key piece sweeps down whole ranks and files. The king is hobbled by the rule which allows him to move in any direction but only one square at a time; Hamm's circuit of the stage and return to center perhaps exhibits him patrolling the inner boundaries of the little nine-square territory he commands. To venture further will evidently expose him to check. ("Outside of here it's death.") His knight shuttles to and fro, his pawns are pinned. No threat is anticipated from the auditorium, which is presumably off the board; and a periodic reconnaissance downfield through the windows discloses nothing but desolation until very near the end. But on his last inspection of the field Clov is dismayed. Here the English text is inexplicably sketchy; in the French one we have,

> CLOV: Aïeaïeaïe!
> HAMM: C'est une feuille? Une fleur? Une toma—(*il bâille*)—te?
> CLOV (*regardant*): Je t'en foutrai des tomates! Quelqu'un! C'est
> quelqu'un!
> HAMM: Eh bien, va l'exterminer. (*Clov descend de l'escabeau.*)
> Quelqu'un! (*Vibrant.*) Fais ton devoir!

In the subsequent interrogatory we learn the distance of this threat (fifteen meters or so), its state of rest or motion (motionless), its sex (presumably a boy), its occupation (sitting on the ground as if leaning on something). Hamm, perhaps thinking of the resurrected Jesus, murmurs "La pierre levée," then on reflection changes the image to constitute himself proprietor of the Promised Land: "Il regarde la maison sans doute, avec les yeux de Moïse mourant." It is doing, however, nothing of the kind; it is gazing at its navel. There is no use, Hamm decides, in running out to exterminate it: "If he exists he'll die there or he'll come here. And if he doesn't . . . " And a few seconds later he has conceded the game:

> It's the end, Clov, we've come to the end. I don't need you any
> more.

He sacrifices his last mobile piece, discards his staff and whistle, summons for the last time a resourceless Knight and an unanswering Pawn, and covers his face once more with the handkerchief: somehow in check.

Not that all this is likely to be yielded up with clarity by any conceivable performance. It represents however a structure which, however we glimpse it, serves to refrigerate the incidental passions of a play about, it would seem, the end of humanity. It is not for nothing that the place within which the frigid events are transacted is more than once called "the shelter," outside of which is death; nor that the human race is at present reduced to two disabled parents, a macabre blind son, and an acathisiac servant. Around this shelter the universe crumbles away like an immense dry biscuit: no more rugs, no more tide, no more coffins. We hear of particular deaths:

CLOV (*harshly*): When old Mother Pegg asked you for oil for her lamp and you told her to get out to hell, you knew what was happening then, no? (*Pause.*) You know what she died of, Mother Pegg? Of darkness.
HAMM (*feebly*): I hadn't any.
CLOV (*as before*): Yes, you had.

We observe particular brutalities: Hamm, of his parents: "Have you bottled her?" "Yes." "Are they both bottled?" "Yes." "Screw down the lids." What has shrunken the formerly ample world is perhaps Hamm's withdrawal of love; the great skull-like setting suggests a solipsist's universe. "I was never there," he says. "Absent, always. It all happened without me. I don't know what's happened." He has been in "the shelter"; he has also been closed within himself. It is barely possible that the desolation is not universal:

HAMM: Did you ever think of one thing?
CLOV: Never.
HAMM: That here we're down in a hole. (*Pause.*) But beyond the hills? Eh? Perhaps it's still green. Eh? (*Pause.*) Flora! Pomona! (*Ecstatically.*) Ceres! (*Pause.*) Perhaps you won't need to go very far.
CLOV: I can't go very far. (*Pause.*) I'll leave you.

As Hamm is both chessman and chess player, so it is conceivable that destruction is not screened off by the shelter but radiates from it for a certain distance. Zero, zero, words we hear so often in the dialogue, these are the Cartesian coordinates of the origin.

Bounded in a nutshell yet king of infinite space, Hamm articulates the racking ambiguity of the play by means of his dominance over its most persuasive metaphor, the play itself. If he is Prospero with staff and revels, if he is Richard III bloodsmeared and crying "My kingdom for a nightman!" if he is also perhaps Richard II, within whose hollow crown

Keeps Death his court, and there the Antic sits,
Scoffing his state and grinning at his pomp,
Allowing him a breath, a little scene
To monarchize, be feared, and kill with looks—

these roles do not exhaust his repertoire. He is (his name tells us) the generic Actor, a creature all circumference and no center. As master of the revels, he himself attends to the last unveiling of the opening ritual:

> (*Pause. Hamm stirs. He yawns under the handkerchief. He removes the handkerchief from his face. Very red face, black glasses.*)
>
> HAMM: Me—(*he yawns*)—to play. (*He holds the handkerchief spread out before him.*) Old stancher! (. . . *He clears his throat, joins the tips of his fingers.*) Can there be misery— (*he yawns*)—loftier than mine?

The play ended, he ceremoniously unfolds the handkerchief once more (five separate stage directions governing his tempo) and covers his face as it was in the beginning. "Old Stancher! (*Pause.*) You . . . remain." What remains, in the final brief tableau specified by the author, is the immobile figure with a bloodied Veronica's veil in place of a face: the actor having superintended his own Passion and translated himself into an ultimate abstraction of masked agony.

Between these termini he animates everything, ordering the coming and going of Clov and the capping and uncapping of the cans. When Clov asks, "What is there to keep me here?" he answers sharply, "The dialogue." A particularly futile bit of business with the spyglass and the steps elicits from him an aesthetic judgment, "This is deadly." When it is time for the introduction of the stuffed dog, he notes, "We're getting on," and a few minutes later, "Do you not think this has gone on long enough?" These, like comparable details in *Godot,* are sardonic authorizations for a disquiet that is certainly stirring in the auditorium. No one understands better than Beckett, nor exploits more boldly, the kind of fatalistic attention an audience trained on films is accustomed to place at the dramatist's disposal. The cinema has taught us to suppose that a dramatic presentation moves inexorably as the reels unwind or the studio clock creeps, until it has consumed precisely its allotted time which nothing, no restlessness in the pit, no sirens, no mass exodus can hurry. "Something is taking its course," that suffices us. Hence the vast leisure in which the minimal business of *Godot* and *Endgame* is transacted; hence (transposing into dramatic terms the author's characteristic pedantry of means) the occasional lingering over points of technique, secure in the knowledge that the clock-bound patience of a twentieth-century audience will expect no inner urgency, nothing in fact but the actual time events consume, to determine the pace of the exhibition. Clov asks, "Why this farce, day after day?" and it is sufficient for Hamm to reply, "Routine. One never knows." It is the answer of an actor in an age of films and long runs. In *Endgame* (which here differs radically from *Godot*) no one is supposed to be improvising; the script has been well committed to memory and well rehearsed. By this means doom is caused to penetrate the most intimate crevices of the play. "I'm tired of going on," says Clov late in the play, "very tired," and then, "Let's stop playing!" (if there is one thing that modern acting is not it is playing). In the final moments theatrical technique, under Hamm's sponsorship, rises into savage prominence.

> HAMM: . . . And me? Did anyone ever have pity on me?
> CLOV (*lowering the telescope, turning towards Hamm*): What?
>   (*Pause.*) Is it me you're referring to?
> HAMM (*angrily*): An aside, ape! Did you never hear an aside
>   before? (*Pause.*) I'm warming up for my last soliloquy.

Ten seconds later he glosses "More complications!" as a technical term: "Not an underplot, I trust." It is Clov who has the last word in this vein:

> HAMM: Clov! (*Clov halts, without turning.*) Nothing. (*Clov
>   moves on.*) Clov! (*Clov halts, without turning.*)
> CLOV: This is what we call making an exit.

By this reiterated stress on the actors as professional men, and so on the play as an occasion within which they operate, Beckett transforms Hamm's last soliloquy into a performance, his desolation into something prepared by the dramatic machine, his abandoning of gaff, dog, and whistle into a necessary discarding of props, and the terminal business with the handkerchief into, quite literally, a curtain speech. *Endgame* ends with an unexpected lightness, a death rather mimed than experienced; if it is "Hamm as stated, and Clov as stated, together as stated," the mode of statement has more salience than a paraphrase of the play's situation would lead one to expect.

The professionalism also saves the play from an essentially sentimental commitment to simpliste "destiny." Much of its gloomy power it derives from contact with such notions as T. H. Huxley's view of man as an irrelevance whom day by day an indifferent universe engages in chess. We do not belong here, runs a strain of Western thought which became especially articulate in France after the War; we belong nowhere; we are all surds, ab-surd. There is nothing on which to ground our right to exist, and we need not be especially surprised one day to find ourselves nearly extinct. (On such a despair Cartesian logic converges, as surely as the arithmetic of Pythagoras wedged itself fast in the irrationality of $\sqrt{2}$.) Whatever we do, then, since it can obtain no grip on our radically pointless situation, is *behavior* pure and simple; it is play acting, and may yield us the satisfaction, if satisfaction there be, of playing well, of uttering our *cris du coeur* with style and some sense of timing. We do not trouble deaf heaven, for there is only the sky ("Rien," reports Clov, gazing through his telescope; and again, "Zéro.") We stir and thrill, at best, ourselves. From such a climate, miscalled existentialist, Beckett wrings every available *frisson* without quite delivering the play into its keeping; for its credibility is not a principle the play postulates but an idea the play contains, an idea of which it works out the moral and spiritual consequences. The despair in which he traffics is a conviction, not a philosophy. He will even set it spinning like a catharine wheel about a wild point of logic, as when he has Hamm require that God be prayed to in silence ("Where are your manners?") and then berate him ("The bastard!") for not existing.

The play contains whatever ideas we discern inside it; no idea contains the play. The play contains, moreover, two narrative intervals, performances within the performance. The first, Nagg's story about the trousers, is explicitly a recitation; Nell has heard it often, and so, probably, has the audience; it is a vaudeville standby. Nagg's performance, like a production of *King Lear,* whose story we know, must therefore be judged solely as a performance. Its quality, alas, discourages even him ("I tell this story worse and worse"), and Nell too is not amused, being occupied with thoughts of her own, about the sand at the bottom of Lake Como. The other is Hamm's huffe-snuffe narrative, also a recitation, since we are to gather that he has been composing it beforehand, in his head. This time we do not know the substance of the tale, but contemplate in diminishing perspective an actor who has memorized a script which enjoins him to imitate a man who has devised and memorized a script:

> The man came crawling towards me, on his belly. Pale, wonderfully pale and thin, he seemed on the point of—(*Pause. Normal tone.*) No, I've done that bit.

Later on he incorporates a few critical reflections: "Nicely put, that," or "There's English for you." This technician's narcissism somewhat disinfects the dreadful tale. All Hamm's satisfactions come from dramatic self-contemplation, and as he towers before us, devoid of mercy, it is to some ludicrous stage villain that he assimilates himself, there on the stage, striking a stage-Barabbas pose ("Sometimes I go about and poison wells"). It is to this that life as play-acting comes.

> In the end he asked me would I consent to take in the child as well—if he were still alive. (*Pause.*) It was the moment I was waiting for. (*Pause.*) Would I consent to take in the child. . . . (*Pause.*) I can see him still, down on his knees, his hands flat on the ground, glaring at me with his mad eyes, in defiance of my wishes.

"It was the moment I was waiting for": the satisfaction this exudes is considerably less sadistic than dramatic, and the anticlimax into which the long performance immediately topples would try a creator's soul, not a maniac's:

> I'll soon have finished with this story. (*Pause.*) Unless I bring in other characters. (*Pause.*) But where would I find them? (*Pause.*) Where would I look for them? (*Pause. He whistles. Enter Clov.*) Let us pray to God.

So the hooks go in. There is no denying what Beckett called in a letter to Alan Schneider "the power of the text to claw." It strikes, however, its unique precarious balance between rage and art, immobilizing all characters but one, rotating before us for ninety unbroken minutes the surfaces of Nothing, always designedly faltering on the brink of utter insignificance into which nevertheless we cannot but project so many awful significances: theater reduced to its elements in order that theatricalism may explore without mediation its own boundaries: a bleak unforgettable tour de force and probably its author's single most remarkable work.

Hamm, Clov, and Dramatic Method in *Endgame*

Antony Easthope

One way in which a play holds the attention of an audience for the duration of its performance is by presenting an action which may be formulated as a question: Who killed Laius? How will Hamlet revenge his father? *Endgame* has a plot at least to the extent that it holds its audience with an uncertainty, one which is continuously reiterated from the stage: Will Clov leave Hamm? At the end, when the final tableau shows Clov standing there, with umbrella, raincoat, and bag, unable to stay and unable to go, the question remains unresolved. Nevertheless, any discussion of *Endgame,* including one which proposes to consider the play's dramatic method, should begin with this question, or rather with the relationship between Hamm and Clov from which it arises. And since Clov is for the most part a passive victim, a pawn dominated by Hamm's active mastery, it is with Hamm that we should start.

In order to get even as far as the play will let us towards understanding why Hamm keeps Clov (assuming that he could in fact let him go), we must try to see what Hamm is like. He is like a king, with Clov as his servant, for he refers to "my house," "my service," and even, echoing Shakespeare's Richard III, to "my kingdom." On one occasion he uses the royal plural to Clov, "You can't leave us." In a former time he had real power, or so he claims, when Clov, as he reminds him, "inspected my paupers." Now his realm has shrunk almost to nothing and he is left with Clov, Nagg, and Nell as his courtiers. His relationship with Clov is like that between Pozzo and Lucky in *Godot,* and its quality is well conveyed

From *Modern Drama* 10, no. 4 (February 1968). © 1968 by A. C. Edwards.

by Lionel Abel's suggestion that it is an analogue of the relationship between the young Beckett and the old, blind, Joyce. Hamm treats Nagg and Nell as further objects for gratuitous affliction—"Bottle him!" Hamm seems to be a tyrant, who lives to enjoy the exercise of his power over others. But it is at this point that the difficulties begin, for to say that Hamm enjoys exercising power is to attribute a familiar form of psychological motivation to him—and it is hard to be sure he has the capacity for this. Together with its many other connotations, Hamm is the name for an actor, for one who creates an identity which has only an imaginary existence. And the tone of what Hamm says is frequently consistent with that of an assumed identity, one deliberately acted out. So he deals with the requests of his servants:

> CLOV: He wants a sugar-plum.
> HAMM: He'll get a sugar-plum.

Hamm's reply is such a fulsome expression of largesse and arrogant condescension that it seems merely a verbal gesture. Nagg does not get his sugarplum, but what we might take to be Hamm's intentional malice cannot properly be distinguished from a pretence of high-handed magnificence which is part of the role he plays. Hamm orders Clov to screw down the lids of the ashbins on Nagg and Nell, and then comments on himself, "My anger subsides, I'd like to pee." It is this continuous self-consciousness in Hamm's words and tone of voice which inhibits us from ascribing his cruelty to an impulse beyond the need for rhetorical coherence in the role he plays.

Hamm appears to suffer, but with this there is the same doubt as with his cruelty. While introducing himself, Hamm proclaims his agony:

> Can there be misery—(*he yawns*)—loftier than mine? No doubt.
> Formerly. But now?

His expression of "loftier misery" is laden with echoes of Oedipus the King and of Christ as presented in Herbert's poem, "The Sacrifice," with the famous refrain, "Was ever grief like to mine?" The salt of genuine affliction dissolves among these overtones into a self-conscious rhetoric, a heavy irony directed at the very possibility of real suffering. Hamm takes the magnitude of his "misery" as guarantee for the importance of his role. On several occasions in the play introspection leads him to talk as though he were suffering, but each time his words become a performance. When Hamm speaks of a heart dripping in his head, he is exposed immediately to the ridicule of Nagg and Nell, who react to his unhappiness as a fiction, "it's like the funny story we have heard too often." Later Hamm tells Clov that he too will go blind one day and find himself alone in "infinite emptiness"—but this again may be seen as an act, a set speech which the stage directions mark as to be performed "*With prophetic relish.*" Beckett has written of *Endgame* that it is "more inhuman than Godot" and Hamm's cruelty earns the play this adjective. But it may be understood in a double sense. In so far as Hamm is felt as a real character, then he is inhuman in the sense we use the word of a man whose actions are so extreme that they seem to place him beyond the pale of humanity. His boundless cynicism may be seen as a desperate attempt to anticipate the cruelty of a universe which is indifferent to his wishes, and his expressions of suffering may be symptoms of genuine agony. Thus, in his hatred of "life," Hamm becomes like King Lear, who, when stripped of all he values, can only cry, "Then kill, kill, kill, kill, kill, kill." To describe Hamm's putative character in such melodramatic language is an appropriate response to the play, for all this may be no more than an aspect of his deliberate playacting. Hamm may in fact be inhuman only in the strict sense of being not human, if the fiction of his role is so perfectly sustained that it excludes any capacity for genuine motive and what we take to be real humanity. Such perhaps is the implication of Hamm's admission to Clov, "I was never there," though this depends upon the stress an actor gives to the personal pronoun. So a full account of Hamm must comprehend both the surface fiction of his role and the psychological depths suggested beneath it. And the main event in *Endgame,* Hamm's story, manifests this ambiguity or doubleness with a clarity which must be considered in detail.

Hamm's story may be seen as a fictional extension of his role, demonstrating clearly how conscious he is of the part he plays. He fancies himself as a great lord, a Pharaoh or a Czar. A father comes to him, begging some corn for a starving child. With enormous complacency the master waits for the end of the plea, for the most dramatic moment, before giving his crushing reply:

> Use your head, can't you, use your head, you're on earth, there's
> no cure for that!

This fantasy account of the exercise of power seems no more than a perfect opportunity for Hamm to practise his histrionic talents. Yet there are many suggestions in the telling of the story which imply that Hamm is seriously involved and that his fiction reflects real anxiety and suffering. For, latent beneath the surface of his chronicle, a tenuous connection of metaphors and phrases repeated in different contexts renders Hamm's relationship with Clov as the hidden subject of his story.

Throughout the play Clov is likened to a dog. He refers to his birth as being "whelped"; he comes to Hamm when he whistles, and the master wears a whistle round his neck for this purpose. Great play is made with a stage prop, a stuffed dog, and once Clov hands this to Hamm with the revealing plural, "Your dogs are here." Clov stands continually, he cannot sit, and Hamm is concerned that the stuffed animal should be able to stand. Like Clov, the dog cannot leave, "He's not a real dog, he can't go." But, as we discover, the function of the toy dog for Hamm is to enlarge his role, bolstering his grandeur by standing there imploring him, "as if he were begging . . . for a bone." Through the figures of dog and beggar, Hamm's relationship to Clov becomes transposed into his story. So also with the reference to a child. Clov is Hamm's child, or at least, Hamm "was a father" to him. Hamm tells Clov he will give him just enough to keep him from dying, so that, like the starving boy in the story, Clov will be "hungry all the time." At the end, when Clov says he sees a small boy approaching, Hamm tells him he will need him no longer, implying that the small boy will take Clov's place. Thus Hamm's violent pronouncement to the beggar and his child is felt as though spoken to Clov. Twice elsewhere in the play Hamm says "Use your head," on both occasions while addressing Clov.

It may be that Hamm keeps coming back to his story simply in the interest of art. For the raconteur practice makes perfect, and Hamm appears to think his only concern with the anecdote is to polish its phrasing—"Technique, you know." But it is hard not to respond to the way he returns again and again to his story as symptomatic of a genuine obsession with it. If this is so, it is consistent with the character suggested behind Hamm's role. The telling of the story looks like a guilty attempt by Hamm to convince himself that nihilism justifies hardness of heart, "you're on earth, there's no cure for that!" Guilt would result if Hamm feared that his cynicism were merely a rationalization for a cruel impulse prior to it, and Clov awakens exactly this fear later in the play, the effect being to drive Hamm almost into silence:

> CLOV (*harshly*): When old Mother Pegg asked you for oil for
> her lamp and you told her to get out to hell, you knew
> what was happening then, no? (*Pause.*) You know what
> she died of, Mother Pegg? Of darkness.
> HAMM (*feebly*): I hadn't any.
> CLOV (*as before*): Yes, you had.

That Hamm's story disturbs him at a level which he cannot—or will not—recognize is implied by what follows it in the rest of the play. Immediately after Hamm's story the famous prayer to God takes place. Perhaps this is another facet of Hamm's role, another fiction, since it is prefaced by his remark that he may need "other characters." Or again, it may be a symptom of remorse and an authentic quest for grace, particularly if Hamm has remembered the biblical parable echoed in his story, that of Dives and Lazarus, and thought of the appalling punishment meted out to the cruel master at the end of that. Earlier Hamm had made a jocular reference to Clov's kissing him goodbye before leaving; after the story the motif recurs, but this time Hamm's phrasing sounds personally insistent:

HAMM: Kiss me. (*Pause.*) Will you not kiss me?

Is this another patronising demand for homage, dictated by the master's role? Or are we to detect in it a lurking desire for forgiveness? All through the play Hamm has nagged Clov for his painkiller; on the single occasion he repeats his request after the story, he is answered in the affirmative, and then told by Clov, "There's no more pain-killer." Hamm's reaction to this seems to be the hysteria of uncontrollable agony:

HAMM (*soft*): What'll I do? (*Pause. In a scream.*) What'll I do?

Yet the violence of this disappears in his next words to Clov, "What are you doing?" Anaphora smooths over the expressive intensity of Hamm's cry, making it seem less a cry of pain and more like a mere ruffle in the verbal surface. At the end of the play Clov's reported sighting of a small boy is followed by Hamm's final soliloquy, which contains a last reference to his story, "If he could have his child with him."

What this argument has tried to show is that Hamm has a double nature, existing both as consciously played role and as real character. His role as king and master seems to be unbroken and self-contained. Any subject to which he directs his attention, even his own suffering, becomes falsified through absorption into conscious rhetoric and turned into the performance of an actor. Yet there is something more about Hamm, which escapes his attention, a network of possibilities, a string of metaphorical connections and repeated phrases, leading beyond the role he knows he is playing. This implies obliquely a psychological reality in him, one which would perhaps evaporate into fiction if Hamm were able to give it explicit articulation. And this ambivalent relationship between surface and depth in the way that Hamm is dramatised is worked out as a structural principle in the whole of *Endgame*. The depths of the play, its metaphorical and suggestive qualities, have occupied the attention of most critics of the play. Hugh Kenner in his book on Beckett and also Robert Benedetti in a recent article for the *Chicago Review* have shown how the play is aware of itself as a text performed in a theater. It is sufficient to list the technical theatrical terms used in it in order to remark the rigor with which this effect is created: "farce," "audition," "aside," "soliloquy," "dialogue," "underplot," "exit." The result of these references is that many lines come to sound as comments on the play made from the stage, "This is slow work," and so on. But if *Endgame* contains a consciousness of itself as a theatrical performance generated according to the conventions of that form, this is only part of the whole. For the verbal surface of the play is pervaded by a deliberate sense of artifice, which never allows an audience to forget they are watching a game played according to certain rules. As Hamm says, "Since that's the way we're playing it . . . let's play it that way." And a principal effect of the drama derives from the deft manner in which a consciously sustained surface, itself a meaningless exercise in various techniques, is held in tension with the expressive significance of what is suggested beneath it.

One of the most unusual rhetorical techniques which occurs in *Endgame* is this:

> NAGG: I had it yesterday.
> NELL (*elegaic*): Ah yesterday! (*They turn painfully towards each other.*)

A little later the same turn is again given to the word "yesterday" in an exchange between Nagg and Nell. A word from the first speaker's sentence is repeated with an exclamation mark in reply. The effect in both these cases is, as the stage directions make clear, to parody sentimental evocation. On another occasion the tone is marked to imply scepticism:

> CLOV (*dismayed*): Looks like a small boy!
> HAMM (*sarcastic*): A small . . . boy!

But when it is not discriminated by the directions the tone of the exclamation must combine contempt, scepticism and sadness. The function of the device seems to be to sterilise an emotional gesture by questioning assumptions it contains. Thus it is perfectly placed at a point when the dialogue discusses just such a movement as the turn of phrase enacts:

> HAMM: We're not beginning to . . . to . . . mean something?
> CLOV: Mean something! You and I, mean something! (*Brief laugh.*) That's a good one!

By the end of the play the device has become a cliché, and thus when it is used twice on the mention of a heart as Hamm and Clov exchange goodbyes, the exclamation has been robbed of most of the force it had as an assertive protest:

> HAMM: A few words . . . to ponder . . . in my heart.
> CLOV: Your heart!

Of course what Hamm says may be a sincere plea for kindness from Clov, just as his reply may be taken to express bitter contempt for the way he has been exploited by the master. But it would be a misreading of the play to respond to the emotional significance of the exchanges without recognising that this is entirely subordinated to what is now a stock response, a merely verbal gesture. The rhythm of this rhetorical device is insidious and easily acquired by a good ear; it contributes a great deal to the unique resonance of the play.

The verbal surface of *Endgame* is aware of itself as being organized in accordance with the conventions governing conversation and stage dialogue, particularly a kind of two person dialogue not unlike that of the old music-hall tradition of the comic and the straight-man. The conversational form admits several kinds of monologue, and these are performed as such. Two anecdotes are available to eke out the entertainment, Hamm's story and Nagg's joke about the Englishman and the tailor. This he is directed to pronounce in a "*(Raconteur's voice)*." Hamm, as the best talker on the stage, has the largest repertoire of monologues. Besides anecdote he is also capable of the philosophic speculation, "Imagine if a rational being came back to earth . . . ," and, with a sense of tour de force, the prophetic admonition, "One day you'll say to yourself . . . ," which he declaims for Clov. In each case the significant undertones are ignored by the surface, so that even Hamm's frightening account of the madman who saw the beauty of the world as ashes is presented as a formal exercise, it being of course that standby of conversation, the reminiscence:

> CLOV: A madman? When was that?
> HAMM: Oh way back, way back, you weren't in the land of
> the living.

The language of Clov's last speech at the end of the play describes with delicate and appalling precision the feelings of a man released after a lifetime of imprisonment:

> I open the door of the cell and go. I am so bowed I only see my
> feet, if I open my eyes, and between my legs a little trail of black
> dust. I say to myself that the world is extinguished, though I

never saw it lit. (*Pause.*) It's easy going. (*Pause.*) When I fall I'll
weep for happiness.

Yet the stage directions insist that the evocative power of this language is
to be deliberately suppressed: "CLOV (*fixed gaze, tonelessly, towards auditorium*)." The speech is, as Clov reminds us, the correct theatrical gesture for
making an exit. For this, as for the other monologues, including Hamm's
self-styled "last soliloquy," the play will accept no responsibility beyond
that for applying certain theatrical and conversational conventions.

The dialogue of *Endgame* is a brilliantly contrived exercise in the art
of repartee. Unfortunately, discussion of a single passage, one of the best,
will have to stand for analysis of a quality of conscious formal elegance
which pervades the whole:

> HAMM: Nature has forgotten us.
> CLOV: There's no more nature.
> HAMM: No more nature! You exaggerate.
> CLOV: In the vicinity.
> HAMM: But we breathe, we change! We lose our hair, our
> teeth! Our bloom! Our ideals!
> CLOV: Then she hasn't forgotten us.
> HAMM: But you say there is none.
> CLOV (*sadly*): No one that ever lived ever thought so crooked
> as we.
> HAMM: We do what we can.
> CLOV: We shouldn't.

The issue behind this exchange is clear enough—whether Nature and Nature's God have temporarily withdrawn themselves from man or have
actually ceased to exist. But serious concern with this question is submerged
in this sharp, witty, paradoxical dialogue, often dependent on the interplay
of verbal connection and logical nonsequitur, which is of a kind that has
fascinated the Irish from Swift to Shaw. Hamm's straight-man assertion
provokes Clov's stock response, "There's no more Nature." His denial is
categorical in form, an either/or, but Hamm impossibly calls it an exag-
geration, at the same time employing a rhetorical exclamation made familiar
by the rest of the play. Hamm's response, instead of collapsing the conversation, elicits an equally impossible concession from Clov, "In the vicinity," as though Nature, if it existed, could exist locally but not
universally. This Hamm ignores, launching into the vigorous if paradoxical
proof that universal decay is evidence for Nature's continued existence.

Instead of replying to this in terms consistent with his previous denial, Clov counters wittily by accepting the existence of human decay as evidence of Nature's benevolence, "Then she hasn't forgotten us." Hamm takes this to be Clov's admission that he was wrong, a move which Clov tries to thwart with a sententious aphorism, "No one that ever lived thought so crooked as we." Hamm pounces on this by implying that crooked thinking is all to the good. But his words are ambiguous, for "can" here means both "the best we can" and "what we have to do." Thus the Parthian shaft comes from Clov, who outwits Hamm by repeating his disapproval of crooked thinking in a way which supposes that people do by choice what Hamm has unintentionally said they do by necessity. After a pause, this vigorous little canter earns Clov his master's praise, "You're a bit of all right, aren't you?" This adapts the vulgar British phrase as admiration for Clov's high technical proficiency in playing games with a concept whose varying definitions have worried thinkers of our civilization for over two thousand years. It is because of a similar delight in technical expertise that Hamm on a later occasion cannot resist self-congratulation:

CLOV: Do you believe in the life to come?
HAMM: Mine was always that. (*Exit Clov.*) Got him that time!

Once again, a serious subject, the fate of man's external soul, is used mainly as an occasion for repartee, and this juxtaposition of a formal surface with serious, often terrifying depths accounts for much of what Beckett in his correspondence with Alan Schneider referred to as "the power of the text to claw."

A word frequently applied to Beckett's work is "poetic." What the adjective really points to in Beckett's plays (a context in which it is perjorative if it replaces the honorific qualification "dramatic") is the extraordinary ability of the language and stagecraft to imply, suggest, connote, evoke, and set off expressive nuances. In this respect *Endgame* fulfills expectations which derive to us from our experience of the symbolist tradition in poetry and drama, for it was Mallarmé's principle that "to name is to destroy; to suggest is to create." It is this, and the traditional assumption that drama imitates a reality beyond itself, which Beckett has chosen to exploit. And he exploits it by providing the play with a level of action, which ignores its own significant implications. The surface of *Endgame* insists upon itself as a meaningless technical exercise of the medium in its own right and refuses to acknowledge anything beyond its own expertise. Beckett stresses this in his own comment on the play, again in a letter to Alan Schneider:

> My work is a matter of fundamental sounds (no joke intended) made as fully as possible, and I accept responsibility for nothing else. If people want to have headaches among the overtones, let them. And provide their own aspirin. Hamm as stated, and Clov as stated, together as stated, nec tecum sine te, in such a place, and in such a world, that's all I can manage, more than I could.

The life of *Endgame* is in the tension it creates by the harsh juxtaposition of the depths and the surface, the "overtones" and what is stated, a doubleness which is apparent in the frequent pauses in the play. On the one hand these are hushed silences in which the resonances of the text may vibrate and amplify in the mind of the audience—"God," "light," "Nature," "ended." At the same time these pauses are merely technical requirements, rests between moves in the last game which is *Endgame*, no more, no less. Thus the dramatic structure of the play enacts a dialectic which Beckett has stated elsewhere—in *Watt*, his second novel—as, "this pursuit of meaning, in this indifference to meaning." In so far as we recognise this as an insight into the conditions of human existence we will be able to respond to the full effect of *Endgame*.

Ending the Waiting Game:
A Reading of Beckett's *Endgame*

Stanley Cavell

Various keys to its interpretation are in place: "Endgame" is a term of chess; the name Hamm is shared by Noah's cursed son, it titles a kind of actor, it starts recalling Hamlet. But no interpretation I have seen details the textual evidence for these relations nor shows how the play's meaning opens with them. Without this, we will have a general impression of the play, one something like this: Beckett's perception is of a "meaningless universe" and language in his plays "serves to express the breakdown, the disintegration of language"—by, one gathers, itself undergoing disintegration. Such descriptions are usual in the discussions of Beckett I am aware of, but are they anything more than impositions from an impression of fashionable philosophy?

Martin Esslin, from whom I was just quoting, applauds Beckett for his veridical registering of the modern world. Georg Lukács deplores Beckett as an instance of the modernist writer who, while accurately registering something about our world, fails to see that his response to that world (in subjectivity, angst, formalism, psychopathology) is chosen, and partial— in particular, a choice against a socialist perspective from which alone possibilities for the future of human society can be spoken for by artists (*Realism in Our Time*). One recognizes the sorts of production which fit Lukács's descriptions, the amusements which sell the world its own weirdness. Both Esslin and Lukács take Beckett's work much as any corrupted audience takes it, except that Lukács maintains the classical demand of art, that the artist achieve perspective which grants independence from the world within which he is centered; that he not allow himself merely to pander to the world, becoming one of its typical phenomena, but that he witness it, helping the world to see its phenomena by providing his perspective. Esslin speaks with those who have forgotten that such a perspective is necessary, or who assume that it is no longer possible. Lukács proposes to bring society and art back together by demanding that the artist's perspective be provided by a particular social attitude or choice. Both views are blind to the fact that in modernist arts the achievement of the autonomy of the object is a *problem*—the artistic problem. Autonomy is no longer provided by the conventions of an art, for the modernist artist has continuously to question the conventions upon which his art has depended; nor is it furthered by any position the artist can adopt, towards anything but his art. (Contrariwise, the success of socialism is not to be measured by its providing artists with perspective, but by its providing conditions under which artists are free to find their own, without punishing eccentricity or isolation, and in which the members of his community are each in a position to expose themselves to those discoveries, or not to.)

Neither Esslin's praise nor Lukács's blame ought to guide or to depress us, for the former does not see the problem and the latter does not see Beckett's solution to the problem. The first critical problem is to discover how Beckett's objects mean at all, the original source of their conviction for us, if they have conviction. My argument will be that Beckett, in *Endgame,* is not marketing subjectivity, popularizing angst, amusing and thereby excusing us with pictures of our psychopathology; he is outlining the facts—of mind, of community—which show why these have become our pastimes. The discovery of *Endgame,* both in topic and technique, is not the failure of meaning (if that means the lack of meaning) but its total, even totalitarian, success—our inability *not* to mean what we are given to mean.

I

Who are these people? Where are they, and how did they get there? What can illuminate their mood of bewilderment as well as their mood of appalling comprehension? What is the source of their ugly power over one another, and of their impotence? What gives to their conversation its sound, at once of madness and of plainness?

I begin with two convictions. The first is that the ground of the play's quality is the *ordinariness* of its events. It is true that what we are given to see are two old people sticking half up out of trash cans, and an extraordinarily garbed blind paraplegic who imposes bizarre demands on the only person who can carry them out, the only inhabitant of that world who has remaining to him the power of motion. But take a step back from the bizarrerie and they are simply a family. Not just any family perhaps, but then every unhappy family is unhappy in its own way—gets in its own way in its own way. The old father and mother with no useful functions anymore are among the waste of society, dependent upon the generation they have bred, which in turn resents them for their uselessness and dependency. They do what they can best do: they bicker and reminisce about happier days. And they comfort one another as best they can, not necessarily out of love, nor even habit (this love and this habit may never have been formed) but out of the knowledge that they were both there, they have been through it together, like comrades in arms, or passengers on the same wrecked ship; and a life, like a disaster, seems to need going over and over in reminiscence, even if that is what makes it disastrous. One of their fondest memories seems to be the time their tandem bicycle crashed and they lost their legs: their past, their pain, has become their entertainment, their pastime. Comfort may seem too strong a term. One of them can, or could, scratch the other where the itch is out of reach, and Nagg will tolerate Nell's girlish rerhapsodizing the beauties of Lake Como if she will bear his telling again his favorite funny story. None of this is very *much* comfort perhaps, but then there never is very *much* comfort.

The old are also good at heaping curses on their young and at controlling them through guilt, the traditional weapons of the weak and dependent. Nagg uses the most ancient of all parental devices, claiming that something is due him from his son for the mere fact of having begot him. Why that should ever have seemed, and still seem, something in itself to be ·grateful for is a question of world-consuming mystery—but Hamm ought to be the least likely candidate for its effect, wanting nothing more than to wrap up and send back the gift of life. (His problem, as with any child, is to find out where it came from.) Yet he keeps his father in his house, and lays on his adopted son Clov the same claim to gratitude ("It was I was a Father to you"). Like his father, powerless to walk, needing to tell stories, he masks his dependence with bullying—the most versatile of techniques, masking also the requirements of loyalty, charity, magnanimity. All the characters are bound in the circle of tyranny, the most familiar of family circles.

Take another step back and the relationship between Hamm and his son-servant-lover Clov shows its dominance. It is, again, an ordinary neurotic relationship, in which both partners wish nothing more than to end it, but in which each is incapable of taking final steps because its end presents itself to them as the end of the world. So they remain together, each helpless in everything save to punish the other for his own helplessness, and play the consuming game of manipulation, the object of which is to convince the other that you yourself do not need to play. But any relationship of absorbing importance will form a world, as the personality does. And a critical change in either will change the world. The world of the happy man is different from the world of the unhappy man, says Wittgenstein in the *Tractatus*. And the world of the child is different from the world of the grown-up, and that of the sick from that of the well, and the mad from the unmad. This is why a profound change of consciousness presents itself as a revelation, why it is so difficult, why its anticipation will seem the destruction of the world: even where it is a happy change, a world is always lost. I do not insist upon its appearing a homosexual relationship, although the title of the play just possibly suggests a practice typical of male homosexuality, and although homosexuality figures in the play's obsessive goal of sterility—the nonconsummation devoutly to be wished.

The language sounds as extraordinary as its people look, but it imitates, as Chekhov's does, the qualities of ordinary conversation among people whose world is shared—catching its abrupt shifts and sudden continuities; its shades of memory, regret, intimidation; its opacity to the outsider. It is an abstract imitation, where Chekhov's is objective. (I do not say "realistic," for that might describe Ibsen, or Hollywoodese, and in any case, as it is likely to be heard, would not emphasize the fact that art had gone into it.) But it is an achievement for the theater, to my mind, of the same magnitude. Not, of course, that the imitation of the ordinary is the only, or best, option for writing dialogue. Not every dramatist wants this quality; a writer like Shakespeare can get it whenever he wants it. But to insist upon the ordinary, keep its surface and its rhythm, sets a powerful device. An early movie director, René Clair I believe, remarked that if a person were shown a film of an ordinary whole day in his life, he would go mad. One thinks, perhaps, of Antonioni. At least he and Beckett have discovered new artistic resource in the fact of boredom; not as a topic merely, but as a dramatic technique. To miss the ordinariness of the lives in *Endgame* is to avoid the extraordinariness (and ordinariness) of our own.

II

I said there are two specific convictions from which my interpretation proceeds. The second also concerns, but more narrowly, the language Beckett has discovered or invented; not now its use in dialogue, but its grammar, its particular way of making sense, especially the quality it has of what I will call *hidden literality*. The words strew obscurities across our path and seem willfully to thwart comprehension; and then time after time we discover that their meaning has been missed only because it was so utterly bare—totally, therefore unnoticeably, in view. Such a discovery has the effect of showing us that it is *we* who had been willfully uncomprehending, misleading ourselves in demanding further, or other, meaning where the meaning was nearest. Many instances will come to light as we proceed, but an example or two may help at the outset.

At several points through the play the names God and Christ appear, typically in a form of words which conventionally expresses a curse. They are never, however, used (by the character saying them, of course) to curse, but rather in perfect literalness. Here are two instances: "What in God's name could there be on the horizon?"; "Catch him [a flea] for the love of God." In context, the first instance shows Hamm really asking whether anything on the horizon is appearing in God's name, as his sign or at his bidding; and the second instance really means that if you love God, have compassion for him, you will catch and kill the flea. Whether one will be convinced by such readings will depend upon whether one is convinced by the interpretation to be offered of the play as a whole, but they immediately suggest one motive in Beckett's uncovering of the literal: it removes curses, the curses under which the world is held. One of our special curses is that we can use the name of God naturally only to curse, take it only in vain. Beckett removes this curse by converting the rhetoric of cursing; not, as traditionally, by using the name in prayer (*that* alternative, as is shown explicitly elsewhere in the play, is obviously no longer open to us) but by turning its formulas into declarative utterances, ones of pure denotation—using the sentences "cognitively," as the logical positivists used to put it. Beckett (along with other philosophers recognizable as existentialist) shares with positivism its wish to escape connotation, rhetoric, the noncognitive, the irrationality and awkward memories of ordinary language, in favor of the directly verifiable, the isolated and perfected present. Only Beckett sees how infinitely difficult this escape will be. Positivism said that statements about God are meaningless; Beckett shows that they mean too damned much.

To undo curses is just one service of literalization; another is to unfix clichés and idioms:

HAMM: Did you ever think of one thing?
CLOV: Never.

The expected response to Hamm's question would be, "What?"; but that answer would accept the question as the cliché conversational gambit it appears to be. Clov declines the move and brings the gesture to life by taking it literally. His answer means that he has always thought only of *many* things, and in this I hear a confession of failure in following Christ's injunction to take no thought for your life, what ye shall eat, or what ye shall drink; nor yet for your body, nor for tomorrow—the moral of which is that "thine eye be single." Perhaps I hallucinate. Yet the Sermon on the Mount makes explicit appearance in the course of the play, as will emerge. Our concerns with God have now become the greatest clichés of all, and here is another curse to be undone.

> CLOV: Do you believe in the life to come?
> HAMM: Mine was always that.

Hamm knows he's made a joke and, I suppose, knows that the joke is on us; but at least the joke momentarily disperses the "belief" in the cliché "life to come," promised on any Sunday radio. And it is a terribly sad joke—that the life we are living is not our life, or not alive. Or perhaps it's merely that the joke is old, itself a cliché. Christ told it to us, that this life is nothing. The punch line, the knock-out punch line, is that there is no other but this to come, that the life of waiting for life to come is all the life ever to come. We don't laugh; but if we could, or if we could stop finding it funny, then perhaps life would come to life, or anyway the life of life to come would end. (Clov, at one point, asks Hamm: "Don't we laugh?", not because he feels like it, but out of curiosity. In her longest speech Nell says: "Nothing is funnier than unhappiness . . . It's like the funny story we have heard too often, we still find it funny, but we don't laugh any more.") As it is, we've heard it all, seen it all too often, heard the promises, seen the suffering repeated in the same words and postures, and they are like any words which have been gone over so much that they are worn strange. We don't laugh, we don't cry; and we don't laugh that we don't cry, and we obviously can't cry about it. That's funny.

So far all that these examples have been meant to suggest is the sort of method I try to use consistently in reading the play, one in which I am always asking of a line either: What are the most ordinary circumstances under which such a line would be uttered? Or: What do the words literally say? I do not suggest that every line will yield to these questions, and I am sharply aware that I cannot provide answers to many cases for which I am convinced they are relevant. My exercise rests on the assumption that different artistic inventions demand different routes of critical discovery; and the justification for my particular procedures rests partly on an induction from the lines I feel I have understood, and partly on their faithfulness to the general direction I have found my understanding of the play as a whole to have taken. I have spoken of the effect of literalizing curses and clichés as one of "undoing" them, and this fits my sense, which I will specify as completely as I can, that the play itself is about an effort to undo, to end something by undoing it, and in particular to end a curse, and moreover the commonest, most ordinary curse of man—not so much that he was ever born and must die, but that he has to figure out the one and shape up to the other and justify what comes between, and that he is not a beast and not a god: in a word, that he is a man, and alone. All those, however, are the facts of life; the curse comes in the ways we try to deny them.

I should mention two further functions of the literal which seem to me operative in the play. It is, first, a mode which some forms of madness assume. A schizophrenic can suffer from ideas that he is literally empty or hollow or transparent or fragile or coming apart at the seams. It is also a mode in which prophecies and wishes are fulfilled, surprising all measures to avoid them. Birnam Forest coming to Dunsinane and the overthrow by a man of no woman born are textbook cases. In the *Inferno,* Lucifer is granted his wish to become the triune deity by being fixed in the center of a kingdom and outfitted with three heads. *Endgame* is a play whose mood is characteristically one of madness and in which the characters are fixed by a prophecy, one which their actions can be understood as attempting both to fulfill and to reverse.

A central controversy in contemporary analytic philosophy relates immediately to this effort at literalizing. Positivism had hoped for the construction of an ideal language (culminating the hope, since Newton and Leibniz at the birth of modern science, for a *Characteristica Universalis*) in which everything which could be said at all would be said clearly, its relations to other statements formed purely logically, its notation perspicuous—the form of the statement *looking* like what it means. (For example, in their new transcription, the statements which mean "Daddy makes money" and "Mommy makes bread" and "Mommy makes friends" and "Daddy makes jokes" will no longer look alike; interpretation will no longer be required; thought will be as reliable as calculation, and agreement will be as surely achieved.) Postpositivists (the later Wittgenstein; "ordinary language philosophy") rallied to the insistence that ordinary language—being *speech,* and speech being more than the making of statements—contains implications necessary to communication, perfectly comprehensible to anyone who can speak, but not recordable in logical systems. If, for example, in ordinary circumstances I ask "Would you like to use my scooter?", I must not simply be *inquiring* into your state of mind; I must be *implying* my willingness that you use it, offering it to you. —I *must*? Must not? But no one has been able to explain the force of this *must*. Why mustn't I just be inquiring? A positivist is likely to answer: because it would be bad manners; or, it's a joke; in any case most people wouldn't. A post-positivist is likely to feel: That isn't what I meant. Of course it *may* be bad manners (even unforgivable manners), but it *may* not even be odd (e.g., in a context in which you have asked me to guess which of my possessions you would like to use). But suppose it isn't such contexts, but one in which, normally, people *would* be offering, and suppose I keep insisting, puzzled that others are upset, that I simply want to know what's on your mind. Then aren't you going to have to say something like: You don't know what you're saying, what those words mean—a feeling that I have tuned out, become incomprehensible. Anyway, why is the result a *joke* when the normal implications of language are defeated; what kind of joke?

Hamm and Clov's conversations sometimes work by defeating the implications of ordinary language in this way.

> HAMM: I've made you suffer too much.
> (*Pause.*)
> Haven't I?
> CLOV: It's not that.
> HAMM (*shocked*). I haven't made you suffer too much?
> CLOV: Yes!
> HAMM (*relieved*): Ah you gave me a fright!
> (*Pause. Coldly.*)
> Forgive me.
> (*Pause. Louder.*)
> I said, Forgive me.
> CLOV: I heard you.

Hamm's first line looks like a confession, an acknowledgment; but it is just a statement. This is shown by the question in his next speech, which is to determine whether what he said was true. His third speech looks like an appeal for forgiveness, but it turns out to be a command—a peculiar command, for it is, apparently, obeyed simply by someone's admitting that he heard it. How could a *command for forgiveness* be anything but peculiar, even preposterous? (Possibly in the way the Sermon on the Mount is preposterous.) An ordinary circumstance for its use would be one in which someone needs forgiveness but cannot *ask* for it. Preposterous, but hardly uncommon. (One of Hamm's lines is: "It appears the case is . . . was not so . . . so unusual"; he is pretty clearly thinking of himself. He is *homme*. And "Ha-am" in Hebrew means "the people." Probably that is an accident, but I wouldn't put anything past the attentive friend and disciple of James Joyce.) In Hamm's case, moreover, it would have been trivially preposterous, and less honest, had he really been *asking* for forgiveness "for having made you suffer too much": How much is just enough? We have the need, but no way of satisfying it; as we have words, but nothing to do with them; as we have hopes, but nothing to pin them on.

Sometimes the effect of defeating ordinary language is achieved not by thwarting its "implications" but by drawing purely logical ones.

> HAMM: I'll give you nothing more to eat.
> CLOV: Then we'll die.
> HAMM: I'll give you just enough to keep you from dying.
>   You'll be hungry all the time.
> CLOV: Then we won't die.

Clov can hardly be meaning what his words, taken together and commonly, would suggest, namely "It makes no difference whether we live or die; I couldn't care less." First, in one sense that is *so trivial* a sentiment, at their stage, that it would get a laugh—at least from clear-headed Hamm. Second, it is not true. How could it make no difference when the point of the enterprise is to die to that world? (Though of course *that* kind of living and dying, the kind that depends on literal food, may make no difference.) And he *could* care less, because he's *trying* to leave. If he were really empty of care, then maybe he could stop trying, and then maybe he could do it. The conventional reading takes Hamm's opening remark as a *threat*; but there are no more threats. It is a plain statement and Clov makes the inference; then Hamm negates the statement and Clov negates the conclusion. It is an exercise in pure logic; a spiritual exercise.

The logician's wish to translate out those messy, nonformal features of ordinary language is fully granted by Beckett, not by supposing that there is a way out of our language, but by fully accepting the fact that there is nowhere else to go. Only he is not going to call that rationality. Or perhaps he will: this is what rationality has brought us to. The strategy of literalization is: you say *only* what your words say. That's the game, and a way of winning out.

I refer to contemporary analytical philosophy, but Hamm presents a new image of what the mind, in one characteristic philosophical mood, has always felt like—crazed and paralyzed; this is part of the play's sensibility.

One thinks of Socrates' interlocutors, complaining that his questions have numbed them; of Augustine faced with his question "What is Time?" (If you do not ask me, I know; if you ask me, I do not know). Every profound philosophical vision can have the shape of madness: The world is illusion; I can doubt everything, that I am awake, that there is an external world; the mind takes isolated bits of experience and associates them into a world; each thing and each person is a metaphysical enclosure, and no two ever communicate directly, or so much as perceive one another; time, space, relations between things, are unreal. . . . It sometimes looks as if philosophy had designs on us; or as if it alone is crazy, and wants company. Then why can't it simply be ignored? But it *is* ignored; perhaps not simply, but largely so. The question remains: What makes philosophy possible? Why can't men *always* escape it? Because, evidently, men have minds, and they think. (One mad philosophical question has long been, Does the mind *always* think? Even in sleep? It is a frightening thought.) And philosophy is what thought does to itself. Kant summarized it in the opening words of the *Critique of Pure Reason*: "Human reason has this peculiar fate that in one species of its knowledge it is burdened by questions which . . . it is not able to ignore, but which . . . it is also not able to answer." And Wittgenstein, saying in his *Investigations* that his later methods (he compared them to therapies) were to bring philosophy peace at last, seemed to find opportunity, and point, within such disaster: "The philosopher is the man who has to cure himself of many sicknesses of the understanding before he can arrive at the notions of the sound human understanding" (*Remarks on the Foundations of Mathematics*)—as though there were no other philosophical path to sanity, save through madness. One will not have understood the opportunity if one is *eager* to seize it. Genuine philosophy may begin in wonder, but it continues in reluctance.

III

Does the play take place, as is frequently suggested, after an atomic war? Are these its last survivors? Well, Beckett suggests they are, so far as they or we know, the last life. And he says twice that they are in "the shelter." Is it a bomb shelter? These considerations are doubtless resonant in the play's situation; it tells its time. But the notion leaves opaque the specific goings on in the shelter. Do these people want to survive or not? They seem as afraid of the one as of the other. Why do they wish to *insure* that nothing is surviving? Why are they *incapable* of leaving? That Hamm and Clov want (so to speak) the world to end is obvious enough, but an understanding of the way they imagine its end, the reason it must end, the terms in which it can be brought to an end, are given by placing these characters this way: The shelter they are in is the ark, the family is Noah's, and the time is sometime after the Flood.

Many surface details find a place within this picture. Most immediately there is the name of Hamm. He is, in particular, the son of Noah who saw his father naked, and like Oedipus, another son out of fortune, he is blinded by what he has seen. Because of his transgression he is cursed by his father, the particular curse being that his sons are to be the servants of men. Clov, to whom Hamm has been a father, is his servant, the general servant of all the other characters. We are told (Genesis 9:23) that Shem and Japheth, the good brothers, cover their father while carefully contriving not to look at him. I hear a reference to their action when Hamm directs Clov to "bottle him" (i.e., clamp the lid down on his father)—one of the most brutal lines in the play, as if Hamm is commenting on what has passed for honorable conduct; he is now the good son, with a vengeance. At two points Hamm directs Clov to look out of the windows, which need to be reached by a ladder (they are situated, as it were, above the water line) and he looks out through a telescope, a very nautical instrument. (Another significant property in the shelter is a gaff.) One window looks out at the earth, the other at the ocean, which means, presumably, that they are at the edge of water, run aground perhaps. Earlier he has asked about the weather, and there was a little exchange about whether it will rain and what good that would do. Now he asks Clov to look at the earth and is told, what both knew, that all is "corpsed": Man and beast and every living thing have been destroyed from the face of the earth. Then Hamm directs Clov to look at the sea, in particular he asks whether there are gulls. Clov looks and answers, "Gulls!", perhaps with impatience (how could there be?), perhaps with longing (if only there were!), perhaps both. Hamm ought to *know* there aren't any, having looked for them until he is blind, and being told there are none day after day. And Hamm ought to ask what he really wants to know but is afraid to know, namely, whether there is a raven or a dove.

Let this suffice to establish a serious attention to the tale of Noah. Its importance starts to emerge when we notice that the entire action of the play is determined by the action of that tale. After the flood, God does two things: he establishes a covenant with Noah that the earth and men shall no more be taken from one another; and presses a characteristic commandment, to be fruitful and multiply and replenish the earth. Hamm's behavior is guided by attempts to undo or deny these specific acts of God.

Something has happened in the ark during those days and nights of world-destroying rain and the months of floating and waiting for the end, for rescue. Hamm has seen something in the ark of the covenant. I imagine it this way.

He has seen God naked. For it is, after all, the most fantastic tale. God repented, it says, that he created man. How does a God repent? How does anyone? Suppose he has a change of heart about something he has done. If this is not mere regret, then the change of heart must lead to mending one's ways or making amends. How does a God mend his ways; can he, and remain God? A further question is more pressing: How does God justify the destruction of his creation? A possible response would be: Man is sinful. But that response indicates at most that God had to do *something* about his creatures, not that he had to separate them from earth. He might have found it in himself to forgive them or to abandon them—alternatives he seems to have used, in sequence, in future millennia. Why destruction? Suppose it is said: God needs no justification. But it is not clear that God would agree; besides, all this really means is that men are God's creatures and he may do with them as he pleases. Then what did he in fact do? He did not, as he said, cause the end of flesh to come before him, for he preserved, with each species, Noah's family; enough for a new beginning. He hedged his bet. Why? And why Noah picked from all men? Those are the questions I imagine Hamm to have asked himself, and his solution is, following God, to see the end of flesh come before him. As before he imitates his good brothers, so now he imitates his God—a classical effort. Why is this his solution?

God saves enough for a new beginning because he cannot part with mankind; in the end, he cannot really end it. Perhaps this means he cannot bear not to be God. (Nietzsche said that this was true of himself, and suggested that it was true of all men. It seems true enough of Hamm. We need only add that in this matter men are being faithful to, i.e., imitating, God.) Not ending it, but with the end come before him, he cannot avoid cruelty, arbitrariness, guilt, repentance, disappointment, then back through cruelty. . . . Hamm and Clov model the relationship between God and his servants.

And if the bet must be hedged, why with Noah? The tale says, "Noah walked with God." That's all. Well, it also says that he was a just man and perfect in his generations, and that he found grace in the eyes of the Lord. Is that enough to justify marking him from all men for salvation? It is incredible. Perhaps God has his reasons, or perhaps Noah does not deserve saving, and perhaps that doesn't matter. Doesn't matter for God's purposes, that is. But how can it *not* matter to those who find themselves saved? The tale is madly silent about what Hamm saw when he saw his father naked, and why it was a transgression deserving an eternal curse. Perhaps all he saw was that his father was ordinary, undeserving of unique salvation. But he saw also that his father was untroubled by this appalling fact. Nell, at one point in her reminiscence of Lake Como, says to Nagg: "By rights we should have been drowned"—a line which both undoes a cliché ("by rights" here literally means: it would have been right if we had, and hence it is wrong that we weren't) and has the thrill of revelation I spoke of earlier (it is not Lake Como she is thinking of). But Nagg misses the boat. So blind Hamm sees both that he exists only as a product of his father ("Accursed fornicator!"), and that if either of their existences is to be provided with justification, he must be the provider; which presents itself to him as taking his father's place—the act that blinds Oedipus.

And how is one to undertake justifying his own—let alone another's—existence? One serious enough solution is to leave this business of justification to God; that is what he is for. But God has reneged this responsibility, and doubly. In meaning to destroy all flesh, he has confessed that existence cannot be justified by him. And in saving one family and commanding them to replenish the earth, there is the high hint that man is being asked to do a god's work, that he is not only abandoned to his own justification, but that he must undertake to justify God himself, to redeem God's curse and destruction. God cursed the world, and he is cursed. This seems to me to set the real problem of Theodicy, to justify God's ways to God. Its traditional question—Why did God create man and then allow him to suffer?—has a clear answer: Because it is man that God created; all men are mortal, and they suffer.

The Covenant, therefore, is a bad bargain, and the notion of replenishing the earth is a losing proposition. Promising not to destroy man *again* is hardly the point, and is not so much a promise as an apology. (As the rainbow is more a threat than a promise.) The point is to understand why it was done the first time, and what man is that he can accept such an apology. As for replenishing the earth, what will that do but create more fathers and sons, and multiply the need for justification? God was right the first time: the end of flesh is come, God's destruction is to be completed. Or rather, what must end is the mutual dependence of God and the world: *this* world, and its god, must be brought to a conclusion. Hamm's strategy is to undo all covenants and to secure fruitlessness. In a word, to disobey God perfectly, to perform man's last disobedience. No doubt Hamm acts out of compassion. ("Kill him, for the love of God.") The creation and destruction of a world of men is too great a burden of responsibility even for God. To remove that responsibility the world does not so much need to vanish as to become *uncreated*. But to accomplish that it seems that we will have to become gods. For mere men will go on hoping, go on waiting for redemption, for justification, for meaning. And these claims ineluctably retain God in creation—to his, and to our, damnation. And yet, where there is life there is hope. That is Hamm's dilemma. . . .

Hamm's problem, like Job's, is that of being singled out. Job is singled out for suffering, Hamm for rescue, and it is something of an insight to have grasped the problem still there. Job, presumably, has his answer in recognizing that there *is* no humanly recognizable reason for being singled out to suffer. That is, none having to do with *him*. Life becomes bearable when he gives up looking for such a reason. Couldn't we give up looking for a reason for being singled out for rescue? For certain spirits that is harder, for the good Christian reason that others are there, unrescued.

It is in some such way that I imagine Hamm's thoughts to have grown. It is from a mind in such straits that I can make sense (1) of his attempt to reverse creation, to empty the world of salvation, justification, meaning, testaments; and (2) of the story he tells, the composing of which is the dominant activity of his days.

He calls his story a "chronicle," suggesting that it is a record of fact. It concerns a man who had come to him for help, begging him at least to "take his child in." And we learn that this is not an isolated case, for Hamm refers to

All those I might have helped.
(*Pause.*)
Helped!
(*Pause.*)
Saved.
(*Pause.*)
Saved!
(*Pause.*)
The place was crawling with them!

"Might have." With those words every man takes his life. Hamm is remembering something that actually happened. I imagine him to be remembering the ark being built. It would have taken a while—all those cubits to arrange, and all that food and all the paired beasts to collect. People would have got wind of it, perhaps some were hired to help in the preparations. God, the tale says, went away while it was being done, perhaps to let the family get used to the idea of their special fortune, and to get a full appreciation of God's love. Then he returned to order them into the ark, and when the family and each kind had gone in unto Noah into the ark, "the Lord shut him in" (Genesis 7:7), preserved him, bottled him. At first people would have been skeptical at Noah's folly rising there in the middle of land, but some would eventually have believed, and even if these were the gullible and lunatic who believe every announcement of doom, Noah would have known that this time they were right; but he would have had to refuse their crazed petitions to be let in. Finished, the ark stood there closed for seven days, then the rain began, and some days would have passed before it lifted off its scaffolding to be held up in the palm of God's sea. Suppose it had been built just by the family, in secret. But now the water is deep, raising the general horizon, and the ark is visible for as far as the eye can see, to anyone who is still afloat. Perhaps no one is, but Noah's family doesn't know that. Perhaps the sounds of pounding are not survivors screaming for rescue, only dead wreckage in the water. They don't know that either, but it wouldn't require much imagination to wonder whether it was. They must not imagine, or they must be mad. Imagination has to be bottled. But in Hamm it has started to leak out. He complains twice that "There's something dripping in my head"; both times his father has to suppress a laugh—how comical the young are, so serious, so pure; they'll learn. The first time is his over-hearing his parents together; he tells himself it's a heart, "A heart in my head." Something is pounding. Children will give themselves *some* explanation. The second time he thinks of it as splashing, "Splash, splash, always on the same spot." Now he tries pressing his earlier thought that it is a little vein, and now adds the idea that it is a little artery; but he gives it up and begins working on his chronicle, his story, his art-work. (His art-ery? That could mean, following Eric Partridge on the origin of the suffix "-ery," either the action [compare "drudgery"], the condition [compare "slavery"], the occupation [compare "casuistry"], the place of actions [compare "nursery"], the product of the action [compare "poetry"], or the collectivity [compare "citizenry"] of art. Each of these would fit this character and this play.) Art begins where explanations leave off, or before they start. Not everything has an explanation, and people will give themselves *some* consolation. The imagination must have something to contain it—to drip into, as it were—or we must be mad. Hamm is in both positions.

IV

Whatever God's idea in destroying men, to have saved one family for himself puts them in the position of denying life to all other men. To be chosen, to be special, singled out, for suffering *or* for salvation, is an inescapable curse. Perhaps this was something Christ tried to show, that even to be God is to be completely unspecial, powerless to claim exemption. To deny this is to be less than a man: we are all in the same boat. But can any man, not more than a man, affirm it?

It seems possible to me that this is what *Endgame* is about, that what it envisions is the cursed world of the Old Testament ("Ah, the old questions, the old answers, there's nothing like them") and that what is to be ended is that world, followed by the new message, glad tidings brought by a new dove of redemption, when we are ready to receive it. Without it we are paralyzed.

But I do not think this is what is seen, though it may be a permanent segment. For the new message is also present in the play, and it too is helpless. Immediately after Hamm's first full telling of the story, his telling of it to date, he wonders how he is to continue (as anyone does, artist or man, in final difficulties) and says: "Let us pray to God." There are references to food (not to loaves, but to the bribe of a sugarplum, and to calling Clov from the kitchen), and he finally persuades Clov and Nagg to join him. Nagg wants his sugarplum before he prays, but Hamm insists "God first!"—thus summarizing the First Commandment, according to Christ the first and greatest commandment. Whereupon Nagg begins to recite the Lord's Prayer, taught during the Sermon on the Mount. That occasion is alluded to further in the way Hamm immediately interrupts his father's prayer: "Silence! In silence! Where are your manners?" Christ cautions that prayer be offered "in secret" immediately before he delivers *his* Father's Prayer. If here Hamm's teaching parodies Christ's he will later imitate him more directly, as in his chronicle he presents himself as in God's position, distributing life and death to supplicants. That's the position God has put him in.

The next time he tries to finish his story, instead of praying to God he ends by calling his father. "Father, Father" he says, echoing the repeated among the seven last words, and addressed to the same old party. ("Father, Father" he says again near the end of his, and the play's, last speech.) And now it looks as if he is not only the son of the only spared man, hence has the same ancestor as all men; but the one and only son, with the father to end all fathers. No wonder he is confused about whether he is father or son.

He goes back to his chronicle, to try to end it, or make some continuation, a third time; again he gets to the point at which he is begged for salvation and again this is the stumbling block. Now he quotes the Sermon on the Mount more openly: "Get out of here and love one another! Lick your neighbor as yourself!" And now he becomes petulant: "When it wasn't bread they wanted it was crumpets." And wrathful: "Out of my sight and back to your petting parties." He can find no conclusion to the story of suffering and sin, and no answer to the prayer for salvation, no answer old or new. He has just told them again everything eternity knows: "Use your head can't you, use your head, you're on earth, there's no cure for that!" But they can't use their heads; men are enough to try the patience of a God. "How is it that ye do not understand that I spake it not to you concerning bread, that ye should beware of the leaven of the Pharisees and of the Sadducees? Then understood they how that he bade them not beware of the leaven of bread, but of the doctrine of the Pharisees and Sadduccees" (Matthew 16:11–12). Use your head, can't you? It was a parable! Get it? But he's said that before and he'll say it again, and nobody gets it. They want signs, miracles, some cure for being on earth, some way of getting over being human. Maybe that's just human; and there's no cure for that.

So Hamm renounces parable in favor of the perfectly literal. (People, he might say, have no head for figures.) Only it is just as hard to write his anti-testament that way. Maybe to receive either word one would have to have a heart in one's head. No doubt it is not very clear how that could be, but then Christ sees his disciples' lack of understanding as a lack of faith, and it has never seemed unusually clear what that would be either. ("Believe," said Augustine, "and you have eaten"; Luther thought he understood what that meant.) However it is to come, nothing less powerful than faith will be needed to remove God and his curse, the power to un-create God. Hamm, however, may believe, or half-believe—believe the way little children believe—that he really has got a blood-pumping organ upstairs. We have known for a long time that the heart has its reasons which reason knows not of. But we have come to think that reason *can* know them, that the knowing of them takes over the work of the heart, that what we require for salvation is more knowledge, knowledge of the sort we already know, that will fit the shape of our heads as they are. Hamm is half-crazy with his efforts at undoing knowledge, at not knowing. But no half-crazier than we are at our frenzy for knowledge, at knowing where we should love, meaning our lives up.

Finally, he tries to imagine that it can end without ending his story. "If I can hold my peace and sit quiet, it will be all over with sound, and motion, all over and done with." But it seems to be just the same old story. "I'll have called my father and I'll have called my . . . [he hesitates] . . . my son." He hesitates, as if not knowing whether he is the new god or the old, son or father. But at least he is putting himself into the picture;

no attitude is struck now towards father or son; the son is now not an-other's—as if to acknowledge that all sons are his. "I'll have called . . . I'll say to myself, He'll come back. [Pause] And then? [Pause] . . . He couldn't, he has gone too far. [Pause] And then?" And then a description of confusion: "Babble, babble . . . " (Babel? If so, what does it mean? What caused Babel and its aftermath? Our presumption, in desiring God's eminence? Or our foolishness, in imagining that a tower is the way to reach heaven? In either case the confusion of tongues is God's punishment, hence proof of his existence. Or is the din rather the sound of our success, that we reached heaven and found it empty? Better to bite the tongue than admit that. Better to take over and punish ourselves than to forgo that proof.)

Here is at least one possible endgame other than the act of ending the story: I call; there is no answer. But this ending is unclear. The problem seems to be that there is no way of *knowing* there is no answer, no way of knowing the call was heard, and therefore *unanswered*. (An unconnected telephone cannot be left unanswered.)

One source of confusion seems clear enough. *Who* has gone too far to come back? The father or the son? Is it God who has gone too far, in inflicting suffering he cannot redeem? Or Christ, in really dying of suffering we cannot redeem? What does it matter? The one threatened, the other promised, the end of the world; and neither carried through. We are left holding it.

There are three other allusions to Christ which need mentioning, one at the beginning, one near the middle, and one at the end of the play. The first may seem doubtful: "Can there be misery loftier than mine?" If con-firmation is wanted beyond the fact that the tone of this remark perfectly registers Hamm's aspiration (perhaps the usual tone in which Christ is imitated) there is the refrain of George Herbert's "The Sacrifice": "Was ever grief like mine?", in which the speaker is Christ. The middle allusion is the only explicit one, and it occurs with characteristic literality. After Hamm's instruction in the etiquette of prayer, the three men have a try at it, whereupon each confesses in turn that he has got nowhere. King Clau-dius, in a similar predicament, gives the usual honest explanation for this failure: "My words fly up, my thoughts remain below: words without thoughts never to heaven go." Hamm has a different, perhaps more honest, certainly no less responsible, explanation: "The bastard! He doesn't exist." To which Clov's response, in full, is: "Not yet," and the subject is dropped. Removing the curse, what Hamm has just said is that the bastard does not exist. That Christ was literally a bastard was among the first of the few things I was ever told about him, and I suppose other Jewish children are given comparable help to their questions. I take it this exciting gossip makes its way in other circles as an advanced joke. So it is Christ whom Clov says does not exist yet. This may mean either that we are still, in the play, in the prechristian age, with rumors, prophecies, hopes stirring; or that since we know there is a bastard, he has come, but not returned. (The French version notates the ambiguity: "Pas encore" is "Not yet." But also, I take it, "Not again.") Either way, "Not yet" is the most definite expression of hope—or, for that matter, of despair—in the play, the only expression of future which is left unchallenged, by contradiction, irony or giggles.

What weight is to be attached to this? Do those two words give *the* Endgame to this play of suffering, that with Christ's coming this will all have meaning? It seems unimaginable in this total context of run-down and the fallout of sense. Yet there is a coming at the end of the play, one which Hamm apparently takes to signal the awaited end, and upon which he dismisses Clov. Clov spies a small boy through the glass; it is a moment which is considerably longer in the French, but for some reason cut down in Beckett's English version. In the French, the boy is said to be leaning against a stone, and this seems a clear enough suggestion of the sepulchre. But even without this description, the character is sufficiently established by Hamm's response, which is to speculate about whether what Clov sees exists. (This is the only use of "exists" in the play outside the bastard remark.) The important fact for us is that after that earlier exchange between Hamm and Clov, it is Clov whose immediate response is to prepare to kill the newcomer, whereas Hamm, for the first time, prevents the destruction of a "potential procreator," saying in effect that he cannot survive anyway, that he will make no difference, present no problem. Earlier, Clov had expressed the straightest hopes for this coming, but he misses it when it comes; Hamm is now ready to admit that perhaps it has come but he sees that it is too late, that it was always too late for redemption; too late from the moment redemption became necessary. We are Christ or we are nothing—that is the position Christ has put us in.

Beckett

Richard Gilman

In a nondescript room in Paris during the fall of 1948 Samuel Beckett, who was forty-two years old at the time, began working on his second play, the first he would allow to be staged and published. A year or two earlier he had written a drama called *Eleutheria,* a rather sprawling, unremarkable piece with a large cast of characters which he seems to have worked on in a tentative, experimental fashion and which he has kept almost entirely to himself ever since. After that he had written the first two volumes—*Molloy* and *Malone Dies*—of the fictional trilogy he would complete, once the new play was out of the way, with *The Unnamable.* Asked afterward by a critic why he had decided at that late point in his career seriously to try his hand at drama, he replied that he had been working with some rather deadly materials in the fiction and thought that to do a play might serve as a relief.

There is no reason to suppose that Beckett wasn't speaking the truth, but every reason to think it was far from the whole story. Like other important dramatists, he had turned to the theater only after having spent years writing fiction, and though we tend to think of him as a writer apart, a very special case, he is not so special as to escape entirely the influences at work on one's choice of genre or medium. The stage seems to lie in wait for the novelist, its varied seductivenesses suddenly asserting themselves; one can get rich and famous very quickly in the theater (or be brutally slapped down: witness Henry James); one can feel more connected to physicality, to living beings, after the abstractness of fictional creation. And if,

From *The Making of Modern Drama.* © 1972, 1973, 1974 by Richard Gilman. Farrar, Straus & Giroux, 1974.

whatever the motive, you succeed on the stage, commercially or not, it can mean the end of writing fiction, as it did for Shaw, Ionesco, and Genet, or plays will take precedence over stories, as in the cases of Strindberg, Pirandello, and Beckett.

Since *En attendant Godot* the bulk of Beckett's writing has been for the theater (or for radio or television), and he is surely better known to the public as a playwright than as a novelist. In the case of a writer as austere and ascetic as Beckett, there can't be any question of the potentially easier popularity or greater remunerativeness of working for the stage. Far from it; in one of the half dozen or so anecdotes which are all we possess about his actual life, we are told that when in 1949 he sent the script of *Godot* to the director Roger Blin and was asked why he had chosen him, he replied that it was because the production of Strindberg's *The Ghost Sonata* Blin was currently directing was faithful to the text and because the theater was nearly empty every evening.

There was nothing tactical in this latter remark, no strategic modesty, nor was there the slightest possibility of a pose. Beckett's whole work is about "unsuccess," so why shouldn't that be true for its physical fate in the world? In the dialogues on modern art he engaged in with Georges Duthuit in 1949 (his only public appearance of which we have record) he asserted, or rather let fall that "to be an artist is to fail, as no other dare fail. Failure is his world." The same dialogues contain of course his best-known description of the impossible function of art in the present: "The expression that there is nothing to express, nothing with which to express, nothing from which to express, no power to express, no desire to express, together with the obligation to express."

Beckett seems to have turned to the theater for reasons beyond that of "relief" from the exigencies of his unprecedentedly rigorous prose. Drama is another case of the obligation to express. Like Pirandello, whose plays rose out of the same intellectual atmosphere and metaphysical compulsion as his fiction and were in a number of instances directly based on his own stories, Beckett began to write for the stage as an alternative mode of expression from a unitary source. Neither his nor Pirandello's plays are theatricalized or histrionic versions of the themes of the fiction, but represent a natural and necessary movement of imagination, the extension of a single voice that had been speaking in the monologues of which at bottom all fiction is composed, into dialogue, embodied conversation.

The relationship of the plays to the fiction is therefore extremely close, without being at all parasitic. Beckett once told a critic, Colin Duckworth, "If you want to find the origin of *Waiting for Godot,* look at *Murphy.*" In fact *Murphy's* world of the "nothing new," where there are no high or low points, where everything tends toward stasis and the sun shines because it "can't do otherwise," is very much the world of Beckett's first play. Similarly, the action of *Waiting for Godot,* as of other of his plays, in both a physical sense and as an aesthetic process, is nowhere better described than in the following key passage from his second novel, *Watt*: "Nothing had happened, with all the clarity and solidity of something, a thing that was nothing had happened with the utmost formal distinction."

But the fiction everywhere offers clues, connections, pointers to the plays, is full of monologues that are going to be transformed into enactments, with the different order of recognition that will then be present: the last words of *The Unnamable*— "You must go on, I can't go on, I'll go on"; Molloy's cry—"To be literally incapable of motion at last, that must be something!"; the Unnamable's lament, whose burden is that of Beckett's entire work, fiction and drama alike—"time doesn't pass, don't pass from you, why it piles up all about you, instant on instant, on all sides, deeper and deeper, thicker and thicker, your time, others' time, the time of the ancient dead and the dead yet unborn, why it buries you grain by grain neither dead nor alive, with no memory of anything, no hope of anything, no knowledge of anything, no history and no prospects, buried under the seconds, saying any old thing, your mouth full of sand."

Like his fiction, Beckett's plays are built out of the most unpromising themes and conditions for an enterprise of imagination: occluded movement or outright immobility; a refusal of hierarchies in personal experience or in the organization of the social world; a negation of the distinctive characteristics of objects; a violent mistrust of language; most generally, as he has himself told us in one of the rare interviews he has given, "ignorance and impotence." In his words, he deals with "a whole zone of being that has always been set aside by artists as something unusable," and this is perhaps even truer of the plays than of the fiction. Again, even more than the fiction, the plays follow a descending path toward a destination close to invisibility and silence. His last theater pieces have been *Come and Go,* which he wrote in 1965 and calls a "dramaticule," and *Not I,* written in 1972. *Come and Go* is barely two pages long and can take no more than three or four minutes in performance, while *Not I* is all of ten minutes long.

By now there is a large body of criticism of Beckett's theater, some of it of a very high order: Jacques Guicharnaud's, Hugh Kenner's, Ruby Cohn's, among writings in English. But like that of the fiction, this criticism often suffers from a scanting of the works' aesthetic reality, their mysterious functioning as drama, in favor of their being seen as closed philosophical utterances, histrionic forms of the vision Beckett had previously shaped into intense, arid tales, structures of intellectual despair placed on stage. Or else, if they are accepted as proper dramas, they are made local, particularized into anecdotes or fables of circumscribed and idiosyncratic conditions.

Thus an observer as acute and wrongheaded as Norman Mailer could detect the motif of impotence in *Waiting for Godot* but interpret it as sexual, delivering the play over to his own anxious concerns so brutally shrinking its dimensions. In the same way an astute critic like the Yugoslavian scholar Darko Suvin can call Beckett's entire theater "relevant" only in "random and closed situations of human existence: in war, camps, prisons, sickness, old age, grim helplessness." Yet if these plays are not "relevant" to everything, coherent with human situations everywhere, then they are merely peripheral games of the imagination, grim and transient jests. But they are nothing of the kind.

If such categories as optimism and pessimism pertain at all to Beckett, then *Endgame* is much more pessimistic than *Waiting for Godot*. In its seedy room whose windows look out on empty ocean, the living world seems to have been narrowed down to four survivors: Hamm, who cannot see or stand; Clov, his servant, who cannot sit; and Nagg and Nell, his parents, who exist throughout in ash cans. Everything is winding down to a finish, as in that ultimate phase of a chess match which gives the play its title. Humanly, it is dissolution rather than explicit death that seems to be in the offing. There are no more coffins, we are told; death as a rite, and therefore as connection to human truth, has been abrogated.

In this burned-out world, which has been compared to that of Lear at the end of his drama but perhaps more closely resembles that of Woyzeck, despair is an axiom. When at one point Clov tells Hamm that his father is weeping down in his ash can, Hamm replies, "Then he's living." He then asks Clov, "Did you ever have an instant of happiness?" to which the response is "Not to my knowledge." "You're on earth," Hamm tells him, "there's no cure for that." Only Clov seems to have any desire or capacity for a change of circumstances; he grumbles or protests bitterly throughout at his subjection to Hamm, and in fact seems in the end to have made good his repeated threats to leave, as though from a doomed house.

It is tempting to see in all this a parable of man at the end of his rope, more specifically postatomic man, and the play has indeed been staged along the lines of a vision of the world after nuclear holocaust, as well as, from a different but equally "contemporary" perspective, along Freudian and Marxist ones. But this is in a peculiar way to take the play too seriously, to give it a weight of commentary and social earnestness its imaginative structure continually subverts. We ought to know from Beckett's entire body of work that of all living writers he is the least interested in the present, in the changes time effects, and in what we might call local, temporally or spatially differentiated existence. His imagination functions almost entirely outside history: what is, has been, and what has been, will be, so that writing for him is the struggle to find new means to express this proposition of stasis. In this struggle is one source of the tension of his work.

Another related source is in the unending dialectic between what he is "expressing" on an immediate level in the words and gestures and his obsession with the literary and dramatic impulses in themselves, the human need to say and show. This is his truest subject: the illusion that our speech and movements make a *difference,* the knowledge that this is an illusion, and the tragicomic making of speech and gestures in the face of the knowledge. The materials may vary, like those of an orator on different occasions, but they remain those of a voice engaging in utterance precisely for its own sake, for the sake, that is, of meeting the obligation of making human presence known.

Such materials do not add up to a reassembling of the phenomenal world, such as we ordinarily expect from literature and drama, nor do they constitute a commentary on the present state of personality or society. "He is not writing about something, he is writing something," Beckett once said of Joyce, and it is even truer of himself. What he is writing—bringing into being—in *Endgame* is another version of his Ur-text on the human self caught between actuality and desire, the craving for justification and its objective absence; at the same time it is a drama to show the impulse of playing—by which we fill in the void—to show it up. If it is more desperate than its predecessor, this isn't because Beckett has seen the world grow grimmer or has less hope than before (he had never had any) but because he has pushed the undertaking of artifice closer to the edge, cut down the number of possible ways out. There is not even a Godot now to provide by his felt absence a prospect of a future.

From the opening "tableau," as the stage directions call it, with Hamm sitting covered with a sheet like a piece of furniture in storage, Clov standing "motionless by the door, his eyes fixed on him," and the ash cans adding their silly, mysterious presence, the play proceeds to unfold as though it were the partly self-mocking work of a weary company of barnstormers who have set up their portable stage in some provincial town and laid out their shabby scenery and props. The text they speak has a "content" of desolation and end-of-the-world malaise, but it is interspersed with literary ironies and internal theatrical references and jokes, all of which go to sustain the thesis, most brilliantly propounded by Hugh Kenner, that *Endgame* is a play about playing, a performance "about" performing.

"What is there to keep me here?" Clov asks at one point, to which Hamm (ham actor? the reading is now a commonplace) replies, "The dialogue." "What about having a good guffaw the two of us together?" Hamm says. Clov (*after reflection*): "I couldn't guffaw again today." Hamm (*after reflection*): "Nor I." "Let's stop playing!" Clov pleads near the end; Hamm calls one remark of his an "aside" and says that he's "warming up for my last soliloquy"; Clov says of his departure at the end that "this is what we call making an exit." It is all theatrical, rehearsed, in a deeply important sense *perfunctory;* the scene is not one of despair in a darkening world as much as a weary, self-conscious enactment of what such a scene is supposed to be like, of what it would be like *in literature.*

The importance of this is hard to overestimate, for it is what lifts the play wholly above the chic status of a "God-is-dead" document or an allegory of Life after the Bomb. *Endgame's* thoroughgoing artificiality as tragedy, its self-derision—in his opening speech Hamm says, "Can there be misery—(*he yawns*)—loftier than mine?"—point directly to its imaginative purpose. As in all of Beckett's work, what is being placed on sorrowfully mocking exhibition is not the state of the world or of inner life as any philosopher or sociologist or psychiatrist could apprehend it (or as we ourselves could in our amateur practice of those roles) but the very myths of meaning, the legends of significance that go into the making of humanistic culture, providing us with a sense of purpose and validity separated by the thinnest wall from the terror of the void.

It is not that Beckett doesn't experience this emptiness—no living writer feels it more—but that he is more pertinently obsessed, as an artist, with the self-dramatizing means we take to fill it. The mockery that fills his first plays is a function of his awareness of this activity, not a repudiation of it: we can't do otherwise, *Waiting for Godot* and *Endgame* are saying; we fill the time with our comic or lugubrious or tragic dramas. Still, we have to know that they are inventions, made up in the midst of indifferent nature—stone, tree, river, muskrat, wasp—all that has no question to ask and no "role" to take on.

Thus the derision does not deny the horror or the stress on artifice annul the real. But palpable actuality isn't Beckett's subject, which is, as has been said, the relationship between actuality and our need to express it, to *express ourselves*. Such expression is always "artificial," always self-conscious (since it is consciousness of being conscious that we are impelled by), and never directly "true." "Matter has no inward," Coleridge had said, and it is this truth that we are trapped in, material beings who crave inwardness and have the capacity to imagine it. At its most formal level the expression of our inwardness becomes literature, drama, which, as Ibsen beautifully described it in *The Master Builder,* make up "castles in the air."

What *Endgame* demonstrates is how our self-dramatizing impulses, our need for building Ibsen's castles, is inseparable from the content of our experiences, how we do not in fact know our experience except in literary or histrionic terms. And this is independent of whether the experience is solemn or antic, exalted or base. We give it reality and dignity by expressing it, we validate it by finding, or rather hopelessly seeking, the "right" words and forms. This is what is going on in *Endgame* beneath the lugubriousness and anomie: "Something is taking its course," Clov says, not their lives— they are actors, they have no "lives"—but their filling in of the emptiness with their drama.

"By his stress on the actors as professional men and so on the play as an occasion in which they operate," as Kenner has written, Beckett turns the piece from a report, however fantastic, on the state of the world to an image of the world being dramatized. In this performance the actor is not an interpreter or incarnation of surrogate emotion for the audience but simply the professional embodiment of an activity we all engage in, at every moment, to build the wall against silence and nonbeing. "Outside of here it's death," Hamm says, and what he means is not that death is closing in but that *inside,* in this stage-as-room and room-as-stage, the play goes forward to enact the human answer to it, the absurd, futile, nobly unyielding artifice of our self-expression.

If the true action and subject of the play are therefore the enactment of despair rather than despair itself, then the relationships of the characters to one another have to be seen in an untraditional light. Like Pozzo and Lucky, Hamm and Clov have been thought of as impotent master and sullenly rebellious servant (capitalism and the working class? imperialism and emerging nations?) or, more subtly, as paradigmatic of every human relation of exploitation and tyranny. But once again this is to take their connection too literally, at its verbal surface. We ought to remember that Beckett is not interested in human relations as such but in human ontology, in the status of the stripped, isolated self beneath social elaboration. It is the requirement of the stage that there be at least duality, tension demanding

otherness, that turns his play away from the nearly solipsistic interior monologues of his novels.

Yet something is carried over from the fiction to the drama, and it is
a central clue to Beckett's new dramaturgy. If Hamm and Clov do not
represent or incarnate any types discoverable in the social world, they are
not even discrete personalities, except as they possess a sort of provisional
and tactical individuation as a source of dialogue and therefore of dramatic
propulsion. For many things about the play suggest that there is really only
one consciousness or locus of being in the room, a consciousness akin to
that of the "narrator" of the novels, so that it is more than plausible to take
the room or stage as the chamber of the mind and the figures in it as the
mind's inventions, the cast of characters of its theater. This is almost irresistibly indicated by a passage in one of Hamm's soliloquies: "Then babble, babble, words, like the solitary child who turns himself into children,
two, three, so as to be together and whisper together, in the dark."

Clov would then be an extension of Hamm, the seated, reigning,
perhaps dreaming figure. Hamm has invented a servant to be his eyes and
agent of mobility, as we speak of our senses and legs serving us, and he
has reinvented his parents, turning them into his own grotesque children.
He is now complete, the play can be staged, the desperate drama in the
dark. And Beckett's play *Endgame* takes on still another implication: that it
is an illusion that there are fellow actors in our dramas, we have to invent
them as they invent us; we are all children in the dark, solitary, babbling,
inconsolable. But we play, in this case the *end game,* the last phase of an
abstract life worked out in the mind.

The recognition that there is nothing beyond this last invention except
silence—the scenery trundled off, the props put away, the stage lights
down—is the true source of the feeling of extremity that rises from *Endgame*.
There is no doom impending from outside, no tragic or deracinated situation
to live through. There is only that silence on the other side of the wall . . .
and we are running out of scripts.

Symbolic Structure and Creative Obligation in *Endgame*

Paul Lawley

Bare interior. Grey light. Left and right back, high up, two small windows, curtains drawn. Front right, a door. Hanging near door, its face to wall, a picture. And the figures, covered and uncovered, human but barely human. The inscrutable "brief tableau" which opens *Endgame* typifies the uncompromising stylization which is a characteristic of the play's every facet. Even more obviously than *Waiting for Godot* this play is conscious of itself as a parody of a play. As Ronald Gaskell has written, "it is an art more abstract than one would have thought possible in the theatre, its intensity . . . in the violence with which the human has been stylized." The characters are not only players but also pieces to be played with in the endgame. Games are being played with the audience: Beckett challenges us with such portents of significance and meaning as the characters' names, the picture turned facing the wall, Hamm's veronica and, most of all, the nature of what is outside the stage-refuge. Even the characters' physical debilities—Clov's "stiff, staggering walk," and inability to sit down, Hamm's blindness and inability to stand up, and the "bottled" parents' loss of their "shanks"— though their primary function is no doubt to increase our sense of the body as a wrecked machine, make themselves felt as an element of the play's stylization. As they themselves point out, Hamm and Clov are made complementary, interlocking:

> HAMM: Sit on him!
> CLOV: I can't sit.

From *Journal of Beckett Studies* 5 (Autumn 1979). © 1979 by the *Journal of Beckett Studies*.

> HAMM: True. And I can't stand.
> CLOV: So it is.
> HAMM: Every man his speciality.

The dialogue too, as this specimen illustrates, is even more stylized than that of *Godot*. We seem to be several degrees nearer to the abstraction of music than in the earlier play.

In a discussion of the linguistic structure of *Godot* the musical analogy is frequently invited but here it virtually forces itself upon us. Ruby Cohn notes that in rehearsing his Berlin production of *Endspiel* (in 1967) Beckett used musical terminology—legato, andante, piano, scherzo, fortissimo (*Back to Beckett*). In the same rehearsals Beckett spoke of the operation of an essentially musical "echo principle" in the play: "There are no accidents in *Fin de partie*. Everything is based on analogy and repetition." The "echo principle" not only accounts for the meticulous mechanical construction of the play, the scaffolding around which it was built; it also suggests the presence of a symbolic structure, though one which is operating on a far more abstract level than the usual modernist symbolic structure. In order to investigate the implications of this high degree of abstraction we need to begin with a conventional discussion of the play's symbolic organization. Let us turn first to the most richly complex (though perhaps not the most obvious) of its structural parallelisms. Slightly later than half-way through the play, Hamm tells Clov to oil the casters on his armchair. Clov replies that he "oiled them yesterday":

> HAMM: Yesterday! What does that mean? Yesterday!
> CLOV (*violently*): That means that bloody awful day, long ago, before this bloody awful day. I use the words you taught me. If they don't mean anything any more, teach me others. Or let me be silent.
> *Pause.*
> HAMM: I once knew a madman who thought the end of the world had come. He was a painter—and engraver. I had a great fondness for him. I used to go and see him, in the asylum. I'd take him by the hand and drag him to the window. Look! There! All that rising corn! And there! Look! The sails of the herring fleet! All that loveliness! (*Pause.*) He'd snatch away his hand and go back into his corner. Appalled. All he had seen was as ashes. (*Pause*). He alone had been spared. (*Pause.*) Forgotten. (*Pause.*) It appears the case is . . . was not so . . . so unusual.

I want to place by the side of this Clov's final speech, his *aria di sortita,* which he delivers when Hamm requests "something . . . from your heart. . . . A few words . . . from your heart":

CLOV (*fixed gaze, tonelessly, towards auditorium*): They said to
> me, That's love, yes yes, not a doubt, now you see
> how—

HAMM: Articulate!

CLOV (*as before*): How easy it is. They said to me, That's
> friendship, yes yes, no question you've found it. They
> said to me, Here's the place, stop, raise your head and
> look at all that beauty. That order! They said to me,
> Come now, you're not a brute beast, think upon these
> things and you'll see how all becomes clear. And simple!
> They said to me, What skilled attention they get, all these
> dying of their wounds.

HAMM: Enough!

CLOV (*as before*): I say to myself—sometimes, Clov you must
> learn to suffer better than that if you want them to weary
> of punishing you—one day. I say to myself—sometimes,
> Clov, you must be there better than that if you want
> them to let you go—one day. But I feel too old, and too
> far, to form new habits. Good, it'll never end, I'll never
> go. (*Pause.*) Then one day, suddenly it ends, it changes, I
> don't understand, it dies, or it's me, I don't understand
> that either. I ask the words that remain—sleeping,
> waking, morning, evening. They have nothing to say.
> (*Pause.*) I open the door of the cell and go. I am so
> bowed I only see my feet, if I open my eyes, and
> between my legs a little trail of black dust. I say to
> myself that the earth is extinguished, though I never saw
> it lit.(*Pause.*) It's easy going. (*Pause.*) When I fall I'll weep
> for happiness.

Both passages concentrate on the sense of having been left behind, spared or "forgotten," which is one of the moving forces of the play. Yet there is nothing simple about this sense. In a sketch Beckett wrote after *Endgame,* so similar in its chief elements (the two characters are an old man in a wheelchair and a blind but mobile fiddler amidst a ruined urban landscape) that one could take it as his attempt to write himself out of the impasse created by the finished play, a blind man says:

> Sometimes I hear steps. Voices. I say to myself, They are coming back, some are coming back, to try and settle again, or to look for something they had left behind, or to look for someone they had left behind.

The tone and rhythms, with the accompanying syntactic structure ("Sometimes . . . I say to myself, They . . . ") are virtually identical to Clov's (though the "someone they had left behind" is more obviously reminiscent of Hamm's mad painter). But the *Endgame* situation is rather more complex. The stage-picture of *Theatre I*—"Street corner. Ruins"—might be taken, in the light of the two speeches from *Endgame,* simply as an image of the speaker's mind or of how he "sees the world"—"All he had seen was ashes." He waits, perhaps, and yearns for the reunification which is represented by the return of "them": an image in social terms of a psychological restoration. In contrast, the "corpsed" world of *Endgame* is offstage: "outside of here it's death." In front of us we see only a "bare interior. Grey light. Left and right back, high up, two small windows, curtains drawn." Hugh Kenner's observation is well known: when Clov draws the curtains, says Kenner, "this is so plainly a metaphor for waking up that we fancy the stage, with its high peepholes, to be the inside of an immense skull" (*Samuel Beckett: A Critical Study*). When Clov looks out of the stage-eyes he, like the mad painter, sees the ashes of a "corpsed" world. This outside world is for the spectator not an objective fact—as it is in *Theatre I*—but a datum of the perception of one particular individual, Clov. Thus, whereas in *Theatre I* the "corpsed" world is a given fact—we see it represented on stage—in *Endgame* it is a perceived thing, the perception of which depends on the state of consciousness of one of the characters. We can "see" the outside only through Clov, just as he can only see it through his telescope ("One day you'll be blind, like me"). This is an important point because, turning to the two speeches under consideration, we find that in both cases the sufferer (the mad painter, Clov) looks upon—is forced to look upon—the same landscape as the punisher (Hamm, "they") but *sees* exactly the opposite: and what he sees obviously depends upon the state of his consciousness. The sense of being "spared" or "forgotten" in *Endgame* is primarily a mental or psychological one. In one way it hardly matters if the outside world is as Clov describes it: what matters is that that is the way he perceives it to be, just as the mad painter perceived Hamm's "loveliness" as "ashes," and just as Clov himself perceives "their" "beauty" and "order" as a punishment. This is a play about the alienation and end of the mind rather than the end of the world.

Having said this, we should be careful not to limit the larger resonances of *Endgame* too drastically. A. Alvarez uses Kenner's observation to explain away rather than to explain when he suggests that the play is "simply a day in the life of a man at the end of his tether": "If Kenner is right in thinking that the stage setting is like that of a giant skull, then the play itself is a way of representing what goes on in the internal world of a man suffering from chronic depression." But *Endgame* will not allow itself "simply" to be packed off into someone's head and it will not allow us to get rid of the "overtones" which are apt to create such a headache. As Beckett himself has said, the play is "rather difficult and elliptic, depending upon the power of the text to claw," that is, to tease out precisely those irritating overtones which make *Endgame* more than "simply a day in the life of a man at the end of his tether," or indeed, more than *simply* anything. I have said the play is about the end of the alienated mind, the mind that sees only ashes where others see beauty and order. Yet the hints are frequent and irresistible of a terminal situation which is nothing less than universal, apocalyptic. (Hamm's mad painter did, after all, think that "the end of the world had come.") If there are no alternative perceptions of the universe remaining it is *because* devastation is general: "The whole place stinks of corpses. The whole universe." As Hamm remarks of his mad painter, "it appears the case is . . . was not so . . . so unusual." However we must not lose track of our original observation amongst the overtones. It needs to be emphasized that the central image of *Endgame,* resonant and pregnant as it is, has for its origin and core a particular psychological condition, of which the skull-like appearance of the stage-picture serves as a permanent and teasing reminder. The play presents the end of the mind in apocalyptic terms.

Alvarez remarks that the "poignancy" of *Endgame* depends on the "continual tension between a lost world of feeling, once known and still yearned for, and the devastated present," and that the "glimmerings" of "the knowledge of something valuable that has been irredeemably lost" go to make up a real tragic sense in the play. The contrast between a richly fertile past and the devastated present is certainly an important factor in the play: it emerges powerfully, if briefly, in Hamm's evocation of the landscape he showed the mad painter: "Look! There! All that rising corn! And there! Look! The sails of the herring fleet! All that loveliness." And yet our sense of the past in *Endgame* is not a firm one. Hamm himself harbours ontological doubts:

HAMM: Clov.
CLOV (*absorbed* [He is looking out of the window]): Mmm.

> HAMM: Do you know what it is?
> CLOV (*as before*): Mmm.
> HAMM: I was never there. (*Pause.*) Clov!
> CLOV (*turning towards Hamm, exasperated*): What is it?
> HAMM: I was never there.
> CLOV: Lucky for you.
> > *He looks out of window.*
> HAMM: Absent always. It all happened without me.

And Clov's final speech comes to a climax in the bitter statement: "I say to myself that the earth is extinguished, though I never saw it lit." He and Hamm make themselves a duality, that of light/darkness, which, so far as they know, never really existed. They use it in order to make some sense of their present situation, breaking the existential flux up into contrasting components, and endowing each of these components with a particular moral and existential charge. "Grey light" states Beckett with characteristic baldness in his initial stage-direction, but Hamm at least insists on separating up grey into black-white (without these contrasting colours there would be no chess game), light-dark, often with comical consequences:

> > *Enter Clov holding by one of its three legs a black toy dog.*
> > *He hands the dog to Hamm who feels it, fondles it.*
> HAMM: He's white, isn't he?
> CLOV: Nearly.
> HAMM: What do you mean, nearly? Is he white or isn't he?
> CLOV: He isn't.

> HAMM: Is it night already then?
> CLOV (*looking*): No.
> HAMM: Then what is it?
> CLOV (*looking*): Grey. (*Lowering the telescope, turning towards Hamm, louder.*) Grey! (*Pause. Still louder.*) GRREY! *Pause. He gets down, approaches Hamm from behind, whispers in his ear.*
> HAMM (*starting*): Grey! Did I hear you say grey?
> CLOV: Light black.   From pole to pole.
> HAMM: You exaggerate.

This chain of imagery, which begins with Hamm's comment about his own blind eyes, "it seems they've gone all white," is brought to an ironic climax by his "composition" in his final soliloquy of a line of Baudelaire:

A little poetry. (*Pause.*) You prayed—(*Pause. He corrects himself.*) You CRIED for night; it comes—(*Pause. He corrects himself.*) It FALLS: now cry in darkness. (*He repeats, chanting.*) You cried for night; it falls: now cry in darkness. (*Pause.*) Nicely put, that.

Clov uses the same duality, despite his realization of its falsity ("I never saw it lit"):

CLOV: I'll leave you, I have things to do.
HAMM: In your kitchen?
CLOV: Yes.
HAMM: What, I'd like to know.
CLOV: I look at the wall.
HAMM: The wall! And what do you see on your wall? Mene, mene? Naked bodies?
CLOV: I see my light dying.
HAMM: Your light dying! Listen to that! Well, it can die just as well here, your light. Take a look at me and then come back and tell me what you think of *your* light.

Perhaps the best-known instance of light-darkness imagery is Mother Pegg:

HAMM: Is Mother Pegg's light on?
CLOV: Light! How could anyone's light be on?
HAMM: Extinguished!
CLOV: Naturally it's extinguished. If it's not on it's extinguished.
HAMM: No, I mean Mother Pegg.
CLOV: But naturally she's extinguished!

CLOV (*harshly*): When old Mother Pegg asked you for oil for her lamp and you told her to get out to hell, you knew what was happening then, no? (*Pause.*) You know what she died of, Mother Pegg? Of darkness.

A few moments later Hamm himself takes up the death-of-darkness image:

CLOV (*imploringly*): Let's stop playing!
HAMM: Never! (*Pause.*) Put me in my coffin.
CLOV: There are no more coffins.
HAMM: Then let it end! . . . With a bang! . . . Of darkness!

"I say to myself that the earth is extinguished, though I never saw it lit." Existing without understanding amidst the ruined "GRREY" world of *Endgame,* Hamm and Clov "divide" the grey, the only experience they have ever had, into the white of day-light, rightness, richness, fertility and life, and the black of night, darkness, ruin, aridity and devastation. In doing this, they are both locating themselves in a particular pattern (the darkness, or the near-darkness) and creating a mythology for themselves of an idealized past, a past which is now "extinguished" and which they missed. Their fictive dualism enables them to think temporally in an apparently nontemporal universe and to conceive of richness in the midst of a wasteland. This simple mental system is crucial to the continuance of the endgame.

Even the implied geography of the *Endgame*-world is a mental or mythical geography, relying as it does less on ideas or information than on individual words which light up the otherwise stark grey text. All the alternative worlds are exotic-sounding:

> HAMM: Did you ever think of one thing? . . . That here we're
> down in a hole. (*Pause.*) But beyond the hills? Eh?
> Perhaps it's still green. Eh? (*Pause.*) Flora! Pomona!
> (*Ecstatically.*) Ceres! (*Pause.*) Perhaps you won't need to
> go very far.

> NELL: It was in the Ardennes. *They laugh less heartily.*
> NAGG: On the road to Sedan.

> NELL: It was on Lake Como.(*Pause.*) One April afternoon.
> (*Pause.*) Can you believe it? . . . It was deep, deep. And
> you could see down to the bottom. So white. So clean.

Add to these Nagg's taste for "Turkish Delight, for example, which no longer exists"; Hamm's former subjects "at Kov, beyond the gulf" (and a gulf there certainly is between that past and this present), and Hamm's dog: "He's a kind of Pomeranian." In each case a single word lights up the text with a mythopoeic glow. Both the mythic past and the exotic elsewhere of *Endgame* are above all linguistic creations.

It is not only romantic and exotic words which have a mythopoeic effect. If language as a semantic system can be used to create a mythical past which helps to explain the experience of grey atemporal flux (an imagined fertile past implies a universal holocaust), then the same system will inevitably imply a mythical *present,* an "after-time" of desolation and devastation. If words call forth from the flux a yesterday, they will also call forth a today. Even these simple everyday words threaten to cave in in *Endgame*:

HAMM: Yesterday! What does that mean? Yesterday!

CLOV (*violently*): That means that bloody awful day, long
ago, before this bloody awful day. I use the words you
taught me. If they don't mean anything any more, teach
me others. Or let me be silent.

The myths the language transmits, the myths words *are,* have become
transparent and unimportant in the terminal world: "I ask the words that
remain—sleeping, waking, morning, evening. They have nothing to say."
The related dualisms of the play—light/darkness, white/black, day/night,
yesterday/today, lit/extinguished, waking/sleeping, morning/evening—are
seen for what they are: so many intellectual efforts to mythologize, to gain
control of and therefore to survive in a world of meaningless flux.

The moribund structures make "experience" itself impossible to define:

HAMM: . . . Clov!

CLOV: Yes.

HAMM: Nature has forgotten us.

CLOV: There's no more nature.

HAMM: No more nature! You exaggerate.

CLOV: In the vicinity.

HAMM: But we breathe, we change! We lose our hair, our
teeth, our bloom! Our ideals!

CLOV: Then she hasn't forgotten us.

HAMM: But you say there is none.

CLOV (*sadly*): No one that ever lived ever thought so crooked
as we.

HAMM: We do what we can.

CLOV: We shouldn't.

Clov succeeds in breaking down Hamm's dualism of nature (before)/non-
nature (now) but in the process forfeits his own opinion that "there's no
more nature," so that in the end it doesn't matter whether there is such a
thing as nature or not. The arguments cancel each other out and neither
player wins. But then *winning* the endgame is hardly the point: the playing
is the strategy of survival—itself a meaningless exercise— until the end
comes. The game is language, and the play is about the struggle with this
inevitably defunct tool of perception and survival.

Endgame, then, we need to reassert, is concerned not just with a terminal
world but with the survival of the perceiving and creating self within a
terminal world—a more subtle and complex matter altogether. Wordsworth, the great poet of the relation between perception and creation,

declared himself "a lover of all the mighty world / Of eye, and ear—both what they half create / And what perceive."(*Tintern Abbey*, 11.105–7) Thus it can be on the "green earth," but on the grey earth of *Endgame* the delicate balance between creation and perception (so exquisitely enacted in the Wordsworth by the line-ending) is impossible. Nor is the need and possibility of this balance merely excluded from the play. Indeed what seems to be a decisive moment in the drama turns on exactly this issue of the perception and/or creation of the external world. Near the end of the play Clov, looking out of the window, sights a small boy. He offers to "go and see"; "I'll take the gaff," he adds. "No!" cries Hamm.

> CLOV: No? A potential procreator?
> HAMM: If he exists he'll die there or he'll come here. And if he
> doesn't. . . .
> *Pause.*
> CLOV: You don't believe me? You think I'm inventing?
> *Pause.*
> HAMM: It's the end, Clov, we've come to the end. I don't need
> you any more.
> *Pause.*
> CLOV: Lucky for you.

What is at issue here, as most critics (decoyed by the self-conscious "symbolism" of the small boy) fail to see, is the actual *existence* of the boy. Clov's "You think I'm inventing?" should make it clear that what Hamm was *going* to say was not "And if he doesn't *come here* . . . ," as most critics seem to believe, but "And if he doesn't *exist*. . . . " The game is at its most serious. Making the assumption that Clov is calling his bluff by inventing a small boy (presumably as an excuse to get outside and away from his master), Hamm in turn calls Clov's bluff by suggesting that the boy does not really exist and that because his servant has told him a lie—which he has seen through—he can now do without Clov. Clov's "You think I'm *inventing?*"(rather than the more obvious "You think I'm lying?") serves to remind us that Hamm himself has invented an "offstage" small boy in his "chronicle"-story—thus as far as Hamm is concerned Clov is probably only copying him anyway. The "echo-principle" is here working in a suggestive way, and in consequence it is impossible for us to draw the dividing line between reality and invention, perception and creation. If Hamm's "chronicle" was pure invention, that suggests that Clov has invented the small boy he "sees"; on the other hand if the "chronicle" was a fictionalized version of how Hamm came by the boy Clov, the "potential procreator" spotted by Clov might really be out there. At first it seems that when Clov makes his sighting we, the audience, are in substantially the same position as the blind Hamm—totally reliant upon the servant and his telescope. But if Hamm knows the truth of his chronicle—is it "chronicle" or is it story (he calls it both but prefers the former)?—he may be surer about Clov's small boy than we can be.

The scene of the sighting of the small boy brings into sharp focus one of the most important factors about the play and the kind of response it invites. It is only here, when we need, for our own, conventional spectatorial purposes, to believe that what one of the characters says is true, when we need to be assured of an objective fact which might actuate a turning point in the play, that we become fully aware of the nature of the play and our position in relation to it. For if we, like Hamm (or unlike Hamm?), cannot be sure whether or not Clov is inventing when he reports what he sees out of the window, if we cannot "believe" (on the terms of the "willing suspension of disbelief") this, how can we safely believe anything else he, or any of the other characters, has said during the play about anything other than that which we can corroborate with our own eyes? The grounds of the willing suspension of disbelief have been rendered unstable: this is the essence of *Endgame*—its game-ness. "In *Endgame*," writes Hugh Kenner "(which here differs radically from *Godot*) no one is supposed to be improvising; the script has been well committed to memory and well rehearsed." This may be so, but something needs to be said about the vital ambiguity which is created by the *fact* of an audience. For the characters, words are inert aural blocks emptied of all meaning ("If they don't mean anything any more . . . ") but for the audience, though this aspect—the game aspect—is of course inescapable, the normal *semantic* function of language is still a crucial element. The play only *tends towards* the abstraction of music: it has not achieved it. This is not "pure" game, consequently the conventional willing suspension of disbelief is still an important element of the spectator's response. For without this basic response the essential ambiguity which surrounds the nature of *Endgame* would be lost.

When we look at the stage-set of *Endgame* we are looking at a visual image of the function of language in the play. In a world in which invention, fictional creation, is (as we have seen) always tending to become absolute and all forms tend towards abstraction, language, the only remaining creative medium, ceases to function as a medium, a tool or instrument for organizing and making sense of the perceptions of an external world, and becomes instead a separate self-sufficient structure in the midst of the alien environment. It is fitting, then, that the stage-picture of *Endgame* should represent a "refuge." The functions of language and the "refuge" in the play are identical. Both serve to insulate and protect rather than to mediate and connect. The words of the game are like the bricks of the refuge; metaphorically speaking, they *are* the bricks of the refuge.

> *Hamm leans towards wall, applies his ear to it.*
> HAMM: Do you hear? (*He strikes the wall with his knuckles.*) Do
> you hear? Hollow bricks! (*He strikes again.*) All that's
> hollow!

"Keep going, can't you, keep going!" cries Hamm at one point. The game of language is a hated thing ("Why this farce, day after day?") but existence is intolerable without the refuge it provides:

> CLOV (*imploringly*): Let's stop playing!
> HAMM: Never!

To leave the refuge would mean to leave "the words that remain": "They have nothing to say (*Pause*). I open the door of the cell and go. I am so bowed I only see my feet, if I open my eyes, and between my legs a little trail of black dust." The last image, one of existence outside the world-refuge, is one of slow yet inexorable dissolution of self. Even at the "end," Hamm and Clov are bound by a basic ontological obligation to their hated "cell," which is at once a structure of hollow bricks and a game of hollow words. Existence, such as it is, *is* the game. And *Endgame* itself, with its governing "echo principle," is mirrored by Clov's kitchen: "ten feet by ten feet by ten feet . . . Nice dimensions, nice proportions."

But there is a further, more complex dimension to Beckett's conception of the nature of language in this play. It is hinted at by the Shakespearean allusion in the English version of Clov's outburst about words: "I use the words you taught me. If they don't mean anything any more, teach me others. Or let me be silent." This echoes the speech of Caliban to Prospero and Miranda (I quote also the lines which lead up to the relevant passage, since the juxtaposition of prison and language seems extraordinarily suggestive in the light of the *Endgame* situation):

> MIRANDA: But thy vile race,
> Though thou didst learn had that in't which good natures
> Could not abide to be with; therefore wast thou
> Deservedly confin'd into this rock,
> Who hadst deserv'd more than a prison.

CALIBAN: You taught me language; and my profit on't
Is, I know how to curse. The red plague rid you
For learning me your language!
(*The Tempest* [Arden edition], 1.2)

In both *Endgame* and *The Tempest* the master forces the alien system of his own language on the slave and is in turn cursed with that very language. Language stands as an omnipresent emblem of the master-slave relationship. In *Endgame,* however, language seems not only to represent that relationship but also to take its place *within* it as the master. If we consider Clov's last speech by the side of Hamm's reminiscence about the mad painter, the alignment of Hamm with Clov's tyrannical "they" is unavoidable in the light of his treatment of the madman: "I'd take him by the hand and drag him to the window." Clov: "They said to me, there's the place, stop, raise your head and look at all that beauty." Yet, as he continues, we feel that Clov's "they " are far more terrible than Hamm (whose gesture—"I'd take him by the hand"—is at least one of companionship and goodwill). In fact "they," the tyrants whose evoked values consist only in dead words ("beauty," "order"), seem to merge *with* the words, to become the words: "I don't understand . . . I ask the words that remain—sleeping, waking, morning, evening. They have nothing to say." The words too are "they," silent implacable personifications of dead meaning. The sense of words as people—the tyrannisers of Clov—is even more acute in the French original, where language itself plays into the playwright's hands: "Je le demande aux mots qui restent—sommeil, réveil, soir, matin. Ils ne savent rien dire." "Restent" is perhaps more suggestively concrete than "remain" and "they know (of) nothing to say" is a more explicit personification than "they have nothing to say" (though the English sounds far more implacable.) The two versions of Clov's outburst about "yesterday," present a similar case. (I quoted the English earlier.)

HAMM: Hier! Qu'est—ce que ça veut dire. Hier!
CLOV (*avec violence*): Ça veut dire il y a un foutu bout de
misère. J'emploie les mots que tu m'as appris. S'ils ne
veulent plus rien dire apprends-m'en d'autres. Ou laisse-
moi me taire.

One does not think generally of words as doing something active when they *mean*—and this does not really come across in the English. By linking the ordinary idiomatic "ça veut dire" with "s'ils ne veulent plus rien dire . . ." (where "ils" are "les mots") Beckett nudges the idiom to life and thus creates the suggestion that when words mean it is a volitional act; literally: "They no longer *want* to say anything."

Hamm, though himself a ruined tyrant, is no less subject to the tyranny of language than his own slave. But, as we have seen, he is not so much punished by words as teased and led on by them. They dangle like carrots before him the possibilities of meaning and escape. "To think perhaps it won't all have been for nothing!," he cries "vehemently" when he imagines a "rational being" come "back to earth" (yet another suggestion that the world was once lit with meaning and "rationality"). The desire for rationality is a desire for the agents of rationality, words, still to mean. It is because Hamm is still so attached to words and all their existence implies that they tease him so cruelly. As we have already noted, it is in terms of the individual word that he conceives of his alternative, paradisal world: "Flora! Pomona! . . . Ceres!" Similarly, it is the word rather than the idea which climaxes his fantasies:

> If I could sleep I might make love. I'd go into the woods.
> My eyes would see. . . . The sky, the earth. I'd run, run,
> they wouldn't catch me. (*Pause.*) Nature!

> (*with ardour*). Let's go from here, the two of us! South!
> You can make a raft and the currents will carry us, far
> away, to other . . . mammals!

Mother Pegg is not just described with an allusion; in a sense she *is* an allusion: "She was bonny once, like a flower of the field." Again and again Hamm is carried away by the delusive current of his own eloquence, only to be brought back to the realization that "Ceres" or "nature" or the "South" is just the cruellest trick of the language-refuge, still only words. Language used to be Hamm's slave: he "invented" it, used it to build himself a refuge that would protect him from the devastated outside, and taught it to his slave. But a relationship with language can never be static—"pure" medium can never be pure; now he is the slave, together with his own slave, and words the masters ("The medium is the master"?):

> CLOV: What is there to keep me here?
> HAMM: The dialogue.

The dialogue, *not* Hamm himself. Indeed, Hamm might say of his slave-turned-master language what his predecessor Pozzo says of Lucky, the master-turned-slave ("Guess who taught me all these beautiful things") who at one point appears mysteriously to be taking over again: "He used to be so kind . . . so helpful . . . and entertaining . . . my good angel . . . and now . . . he's killing me."

Thus the two dominant images of *Endgame*—the stage-picture of the refuge and the master-servant relationship of the chief characters—can both be seen as metaphors of the way language functions in the play. But, of course, language can function neither as refuge nor as tyrant if it is not sustained and perpetuated by the creativity of the endgame players. Refuge and tyrant cannot exist independently of Hamm and Clov; they need to be continually and perpetually created, and it is for this reason that creativity stands as the large central concern of the play. Let us approach it by way of the two major speeches we started with.

I have left until now the observation of one of the most obvious and important contrasts between the two speeches: both are about the same situation, but whereas Clov describes it from the inside looking out—*he* is the object of punishment who is forced to raise his head and look—Hamm describes it from the outside looking in—it was *he* who dragged the madman to the window and exhorted him to witness the outside world. Of course Hamm has a dual perspective; now *he* is on the inside: "It appears the case is . . . was not so . . . so unusual." This allows him to have it both ways, for Clov, irretrievably entrenched in his own situation, reveals the "beauty" and "order" "they" show to him for the empty values they are, Hamm is able, even by way of reminiscence, to evince a real belief in and commitment to the beauty and order he once evoked. Clov's grinding bitterness of tone serves to empty the invoked moral positives of value and to leave them hollow words:

> They said to me, That's love, yes yes, not a doubt, now you
> see how— . . . How easy it is. They said to me, That's friend-
> ship, yes yes, no question, you've found it. They said to me,
> Here's the place, stop, raise your head and look at all that beauty.
> That order! They said to me, Come now, you're not a brute
> beast, think upon these things and you'll see how all becomes
> clear. And simple! They said to me, What skilled attention they
> get, all these dying of their wounds.

The speech is to be delivered "tonelessly," but its strength is precisely there, in its tone. The same positives are present in Hamm's speech—yet how different the tone. "Love," "friendship" and "attention": "He was a painter—and engraver. I had a great fondness for him. I used to go and see him, in the asylum. I'd take him by the hand and drag him to the window." "Beauty" and "order," "clarity" and "simplicity": "Look! There! All that

rising corn! And there! The sails of the herring fleet! All that loveliness!"
The unreported (no "I said . . . " to parallel Clov's "they said"), exclam-
atory nature of the phrases serves to underline our sense of Hamm's commitment to the "loveliness." (Note that whereas Clov deals entirely in
abstractions, Hamm evokes concrete details). For once his apprehension
seems to be of something more than just words (though these, if only
evanescent, are rich enough); a yearning and a need for natural creativity.

It hardly needs to be said that creativity in Beckett is not the great
positive it is for so many other writers. But if Beckett and his creatures
can scarcely be said to affirm creativity, neither, on the other hand, can
they afford the luxury of denying it. They are bound by what Beckett
recognized in his "Denis Devlin" review of 1938 as "the need that is the
absolute predicament of particular human identity," a need which ten years
later (in *Three Dialogues*) is to harden into the terrible impersonality of the
"*obligation* to express." That the obligation to express is "the absolute
predicament of particular human identity" is made clear enough by *Endgame,* with its word-refuge outside of which is dissolution and death.

As I have suggested, Hamm, with his poignant apprehension of natural
beauty and order, is the chief agent of creativity in *Endgame.* The loadstone
of his creative impulses, the scaffold about which they all accrue, also stands
as the structural pivot of the play: his fictional "chronicle." This is, in
Beckett's own words, "just about the centre of *Endgame,*" and that its
centrality may be rather more than just a matter of chronological positioning
is suggested by the responses of some commentators. The story is one of
cruelty—Hamm tells how he, or a fictional version of himself, once refused
bread and corn to a starving retainer and his child—but, as Hugh Kenner
notes, the "technician's narcissism somewhat disinfects the dreadful tale."
Antony Easthope observes: "It is the continuous self-consciousness in
Hamm's words and tone of voice [as he tells the story] which inhibits us
from ascribing his cruelty to an impulse beyond the need for rhetorical
coherence in the role he plays." The narrative is frequently punctuated by
comments like "No, I've done that bit," "That should do it," "there's
English for you" and "A bit feeble, that," all of which make it plain that
in his fiction, as in his life, Hamm's values are aesthetic rather than ethical:
"(*Narrative tone.*) . . . He raised his face to me, black with mingled dirt and
tears. (*Pause. Normal tone.*) That should do it," "Yet," continues Easthope,
"there are many suggestions in the telling of the story which imply that
Hamm is seriously involved and that his fiction reflects real anxiety and
suffering." He does not enlarge on the significance of these suggestions,
but a fine intuition of Gerald Weales's (in a fairly early discussion of *Endgame*)

centres on them interestingly: "Occasionally . . . Beckett seems to get caught in his own language. Take, for instance, another of the speeches of Hamm to the imaginary beggar: 'But what in God's name do you imagine? That the earth will awake in spring? That the rivers and seas will run with fish again? That there's manna in heaven still for imbeciles like you?' Obviously, in context, the speech is one about the hopelessness of the human condition in which the first two questions about the natural world pick up a blackness from the third, the supernatural one. The exchange might as easily work the other way. Since Beckett is not likely to be sucked in by the pathetic fallacy (although Hamm might well be), one is tempted to assume that spring will return again and the rivers run with fish; manna, then, becomes a possibility and hope blooms incongruously on the sterile ground where the endgame is being played." Whatever the validity of his speculations, Weales's intuition of a power in the language (similar and indeed closely related to Hamm's earlier evocation of natural fertility to his madman) which is felt to be in some way disproportionate to the story-teller's immediate needs is I think a sure one. Let us consider Hamm's outburst in its context. The chronicle is prefaced—and in a sense intro-duced—by an echo of Clov's first words and two droll puns:

> HAMM (. . . *Gloomily*): It's finished, we're finished. (*Pause.*)
> Nearly finished. (*Pause.*) There'll be no more speech.
> (*Pause.*) Something dripping in my head, ever since the
> fontanelles. (*Stifled hilarity of Nagg.*) Splash, splash,
> always on the same spot. (*Pause.*) Perhaps it's a little
> *vein*—(*Pause.*) A little *artery*. (*Pause. More animated.*)
> Enough of that, it's story time, where was I? (my
> emphases)

The puns are comical, nonetheless they touch on the point at issue, cre-ativity: is Hamm's *art-ery* (his story) merely *vain,* or is it something more?

Hamm is telling himself and his unwilling "bottled" father a story which, though parts of it may be "true" (he calls it his "chronicle," thus suggesting that it is "historical"), bears all the characteristics of fiction, as we have noted. The speech is a long one and the actor is instructed to use two distinct "tones": the "narrative tone" in which the story is to be told and the "normal tone" in which Hamm is to comment on the story and his telling of it. As the story progresses the "normal tone" disappears and the "narrative tone" dominates to such an extent that it becomes increasingly difficult for us to apprehend the specified tonal distinction. The story is about a beggar—like Clov crawling at Hamm's feet for a bicycle; like

Mother Pegg begging oil for her lamp; like Nagg asking for Turkish Delight; or like Hamm's own idea of the pathetic toy dog "begging me for a bone . . . standing there imploring me." A man comes "crawling . . . on his belly" to Hamm's fictional version of himself, begging "bread for his brat," or "perhaps a little corn?" Hamm goes on:

> I lost patience. (*Violently.*) Use your head, can't you, use your head, you're on earth, there's no cure for that! (*Pause.*) It was an exceedingly dry day, I remember, zero by the hygrometer. Ideal weather for my lumbago. (*Pause. Violently.*) But what in God's name do you imagine? That the earth will awake in spring? That the rivers and seas will run with fish again? That there's manna in heaven still for imbeciles like you? (*Pause.*) Gradually I cooled down, sufficiently at least to ask him how long he had taken on the way. Three whole days. Good. In what condition he had left the child. Deep in sleep. (*Forcibly.*) But deep in what sleep, deep in what sleep already?

Ostensibly Hamm is talking to his grovelling subject, and his story enables him to reenact the "great days" of his rule ("I inquired about the situation at Kov, beyond the gulf"). But the instruction to the actor, who should still be in "narrative tone," to speak "violently" introduces a suggestive and fruitful ambiguity into the text, for whilst Hamm might conceivably only be acting his "violence," in performance it would be impossible to communicate any distinction between faked violence and genuine violence. At such heights the distinctions blur and violence becomes generalized and always genuine. In the telling of the chronicle we *know* that Hamm is meant only to be acting out the violence of his fictional self, yet here the impossibility (in practical terms) of the actor being able to communicate fine distinctions is even plainer. How does he—how do we—distinguish the "violent" "*normal* tone" from the "violent" "*narrative* tone?" The situation would become absurd: there is only one "violently." The intervening comments about the weather and his lumbago might seem at first to undermine any genuine passion, yet, paradoxically, they only serve to make the violence more extraordinary by offering such an acute, even forced, contrast to it. Not only the words, but the *changes of tone* are violent; thus the urbane comments interact with rather than undermine the surrounding fury.

The point of this is that we feel Hamm's show of violence exceeds its object—even then and certainly now. Why do we feel such a grave and savage undercurrent to what is ostensibly only "acting?" The answers are within the play itself. We have noted Hamm's sense of and commitment to natural creativity. His "chronicle," itself a created thing, is his chief means of destroying, consciously or unconsciously, that sense and that commitment. To begin with: Hamm berates his vassal for imagining "that the earth will awake in spring," but it is he who has provoked Clov's violent responses by inquiring about the sprouting of seeds:

> HAMM: Did your seeds come up?
> CLOV: No.
> HAMM: Did you scratch round them to see if they had
>   sprouted?
> CLOV: They haven't sprouted.
> HAMM: Perhaps it's still too early.
> CLOV: If they were going to sprout they would have sprouted.
>   (*Violently.*) They'll never sprout.

Hamm belabours his vassal for anticipating the teeming foison of nature which never will return, yet in the play's anticipation of nature the ecstasy is all his: "But beyond the hills? Eh? Perhaps its still green. Eh? (*Pause.*) Flora! Pomona! (*Ecstatically.*) Ceres! (*Pause.*) Perhaps you won't need to go very far." Hamm rants at his vassal for imagining ("in God's name") there to be "manna in heaven still," but it is he who, immediately after he leaves his story, tries praying to God (who is only a name: "The bastard! He doesn't exist!"). And it is here that the parallel between the "chronicle" and the mad-painter speech becomes important, for whilst he raves at the vassal for imagining "that the earth will awake in spring" and "that the rivers and seas will run with fish again," he also revels in the corresponding evocation for the madman: "Look! There! All that rising corn! And there! Look! The sails of the herring fleet! All that loveliness!"

"Where was I?" asks Hamm before launching into his "chronicle." Where indeed; not just "where have I got to in the story?" but also where was I to be found *in* it?" I have tried to suggest by quotation that the answer is everywhere. Exemplifying a technique which is characteristic of Beckett's handling of narrative forms *within* a play, Hamm's "chronicle" exists as an elaborately-worked metaphorical counterpoint to what we see before us as the "action" of the play, at least insofar as that action concerns Hamm. The story has three "characters": the "I" is not Hamm as he was, but a fictional persona who does not "hesitate to end" or, indeed, hesitate to do anything. He takes the vassal "into service" ("He had touched a chord") only because "then I imagined already that I wasn't much longer for this world. (*He laughs. Pause.*) Well? (*Pause.*) Well? Here if you were careful you might die a nice natural death, in peace and comfort." The "Well?"

challenges himself to justify himself *to* himself (Well, *why* did you take him into service?), as though the taking of a servant is the great mistake. The vassal is nothing less than a personification of Hamm's own impulse to survive—we have already noted the parallels. It is because of the contemptible vassal in him that Hamm, as he informs us himself, hesitates to end.

The urge to survive fathers creativity: the little boy left "deep in sleep" "at Kov beyond the gulf" (Clov beyond the gulf?) stands as an explicit symbol of the creativity within himself which Hamm needs to renounce or deny, but which his urge to survive will not allow him to. Creativity is essential to survival. That is why Hamm speaks "forcibly" of the possibility of the "deep sleep" being the sleep of death. His violent fulminations against the vassal, like his evocation of natural "loveliness" for the mad-painter, enable him to have it both ways (as Gerald Weales recognized): he can anathematize creativity whilst at the same time colluding with it.

Eugene Webb writes that "from the context the vassal's little boy appears to be a symbol of fertility and vitality. He was left 'deep in sleep' three full days earlier, recalling the period between the death and resurrection of Christ, whose birth Hamm is preparing to observe, in a purely traditional way, with holly. Both the birth and resurrection of Christ are traditional symbols of the renewal of life, but Hamm refuses to contribute to the revival of the present embodiment of the same force." "Refuses to contribute?" But this is exactly the point. The "chronicle" trails off thus:

> HAMM: In the end he asked me would I consent to take in the
> child as well—if he were still alive. (*Pause.*) It was the
> moment I was waiting for. (*Pause.*) Would I consent to
> take in the child. . . . (*Pause.*) I can see him still, down on
> his knees, his hands flat on the ground, glaring at me
> with his mad eyes, in defiance of my wishes. (*Pause.
> Normal tone.*) I'll soon have finished with this story.
> (*Pause.*) Unless I bring in other characters. (*Pause.*) But
> where would I find them? (*Pause.*) Where would I look
> for them? (*Pause. He whistles. Enter Clov.*) Let us pray to
> God.
> NAGG: Me sugar-plum!
> CLOV: There's a rat in the kitchen!
> HAMM: A rat! Are there still rats?
> CLOV: In the kitchen there's one.
> HAMM: And you haven't exterminated him?
> CLOV: Half. You disturbed us.

HAMM: He can't get away.
CLOV: No.
HAMM: You'll finish him later. Let us pray to God.

We have here an odd but characteristic bit of counterpointing between the stage-situation and the "situation" within Hamm's narrative. The moment Hamm says he was waiting for is also the moment we are waiting for. Will he or will he not consent to take in the child as well? Yet Hamm, hesitating to end as usual, sidesteps the crucial symbolic decision. Can he deny creativity and thus end? Or must he submit to the impulse for survival and accept creativity? Apparently he does neither: instead he starts talking about bringing in other characters and then decides to pray to God. This seems to be merely a bored, arbitrary abandonment of the subject, yet in one sense the fiction is continuing, only on another level—having merged imperceptibly with the "reality" of the stage-situation. As narrator of the story, Hamm *is* a kind of God, and the great issue of his story, whether or not "he" will consent to "take in" the little boy, is directly parallel to his situation as narrator: "I'll soon have finished with this story. . . . Unless I *bring in* other characters." And since he is the God of the story, it is only logical that he should pray to God for more characters ("But where would I find them? . . . Where would I look for them?"). Clov and the rat in the kitchen present a second parallel to Hamm's predicament. As a direct result of Hamm's hesitations over creativity and the little boy, Clov has only half-exterminated the rat in the kitchen. The failure to finish off mirrors Hamm's own. The "climax" of the "chronicle," then, is an impasse. Hamm wants to end, wants to destroy all the springs of creativity within himself, yet he cannot because there is always a part of him which wants to survive, hesitating to end. Creativity is a hated obligation. Nonetheless the climax of the "chronicle" does not exactly disappear; rather it is displaced. Hamm cannot deny the symbolic potency of his own invented small boy, but when Clov seems to be inventing the identical symbol for his master's benefit, Hamm finally feels that he can give up. Again, the "echo-principle" works to confirm the link between the boy in Hamm's story and the boy Clov sees out of the window near the end. When Clov sights the boy Hamm conjectures: "If he *exists* he'll die there or he'll come here. And if he doesn't . . ." (my emphasis: the continuation, as we have seen, would have been "and if he doesn't exist . . ."). Turning back to the "chronicle" we find Hamm doubting the existence of the child which the wretched vassal has left behind: "No no, not a soul, except himself and the child—assuming he existed. . . . And you expect me to believe you have left your little one back there, all alone, and alive into the bargain? Come now!" The issue is one which concerns invention (or creation): for Hamm to reject Clov's small boy outside the refuge is for him to reject the putative inventor ("You think I'm inventing?"). If we take the "chronicle" to be partially true the most obvious implication is that the small boy at "Kov" is a fictional version of Clov. The rest of the play hints as much:

> HAMM: Do you remember when you came here?
> CLOV: No. Too small, you told me.
> HAMM: Do you remember your father?
> CLOV (*wearily*): Same answer. (*Pause.*) You've asked me these
>   questions millions of times.
> HAMM: I love the old questions. (*With fervour.*) Ah the old
>   questions, the old answers, there's nothing like them!
>   (*Pause.*) It was I was a father to you.
> CLOV: Yes. (*He looks at Hamm fixedly.*) You were that to me.
> HAMM: My house a home for you.
> CLOV: Yes. (*He looks about him.*) This was that for me.

And again when Hamm summarizes the "chronicle" for Clov:

> HAMM: Crawling on his belly, whining for bread for his brat.
>   He's offered a job as gardener. Before—(*Clov bursts out
>   laughing.*) What is there so funny about that?
> CLOV: A job as a gardener!
> HAMM: Is that what tickles you?
> CLOV: It must be that.
> HAMM: It wouldn't be the bread?
> CLOV: Or the brat.

Clov is the living presence of the small-boy symbol. When Hamm tells him "I don't need you any more," he is symbolically disclaiming creativity.

But of course Hamm's disclaiming, like everything else at the end of the play, is ambiguous. He takes up the "chronicle" again momentarily in his final soliloquy, but still nothing is resolved, except perhaps the elements of the story:

> (*Narrative tone.*) If he could have his child with him. . . . (*Pause.*)
> It was the moment I was waiting for. (*Pause.*) You don't want
> to abandon him? You want him to bloom while you are with-
> ering? Be there to solace your last million last moments? (*Pause.*)
> He doesn't realise, all he knows is hunger, and cold, and death
> to crown it all. But you! You ought to know what the earth is

like nowadays. Oh, I put him before his responsibilities! (*Pause. Normal tone.*) Well, there we are, there I am, that is enough.

There he is indeed. And there is Clov *"impassive and motionless, his eyes fixed on Hamm, till the end."* The way the text mirrors the stage-situation is now clearer than ever. The characters seem almost to merge into their fictions: Hamm into the vassal, Clov into the small boy; Hamm withering and Clov solacing his father's last million last moments. The "chronicle" can now be seen for what it always was: an expanded image of Hamm's own creative situation.

"But if the occasion appears as an unstable term of relation, the artist, who is the other term, is hardly less so, thanks to his warren of modes and attitudes." This, from *Three Dialogues,* might be a gloss on Hamm, than whom no Beckett character, unless it be Winnie in *Happy Days,* has a more extensive and thoroughly explored warren of modes and attitudes. Hugh Kenner, in a review of *Ends and Odds* (1977), maintains that Beckett's plays "work by locating the most lyrical or the most outrageous sentiment firmly within the compass of an alien voice—the kind of thing *he* says—and then letting the voice multiply voices, create more characters, till the voice we first heard seems but another creation and the sentiment is dispersed by a wilderness of mirrors. 'Can there be misery . . . loftier than mine?' That was Hamm, hamming, and later Hamm becomes the fantasist of a dreadful tale in which peasants (*sic*) crawl toward him on their bellies. Then wasn't the Hamm we first heard a fantasy too? His own? Whose?" As Kenner's questions suggest, Hamm himself is not a "stable term." I said that he was Everywhere in his story, and yet, because all those versions of himself are incomplete, imperfect, there is a sense in which he is Nowhere. What, for example, do we see in front of us on the stage? [As Hugh Kenner comments in *Critical Study*], Hamm is, as his name suggests, the type of the Actor, "a creature all circumference and no center." He is *made up* of his "stiff toque" and whistle, his dressing gown, his rug, his thick socks, his black glasses and his sudarium, placed "more or less" "roughly" "right in the centre" of the stage, assuming his various "modes and attitudes." Even more obviously than any of the characters in *Godot* (save perhaps his immediate ancestor Pozzo), Hamm's, to use Alain Robbe-Grillet's fine phrase, a "provisional being." His presence is not authentic, completed, but the *parody* presence of the Actor.

Endgame is full of things imperfect or unfinished: the half-exterminated rat; the nearly-white dog which "isn't finished" (the sex goes on at the end); Hamm's "chronicle" itself ("I'll soon have finished with this story");

his image of "the millet grains of . . . that old Greek"—"all life long you wait for that to mount up to a life"; the physical states of all the characters, and the endgame itself. ("Old stancher . . . You . . . remain.") The play's opening words—"finished, it's finished, nearly finished, it must be nearly finished"—are also its most poignantly ironic ones. The dog, the "chronicle," the game itself are all creations: they are not just imperfect but imperfectly *created*. Hamm invents images, stories and fantasies because, in order to survive against the threatening outside ("outside of here it's death"), he is obliged to create himself; he is perpetually attempting to "finish off" a self imperfectly created and therefore existing only in a parodic dimension, a "parody presence."

Though it is less obvious here than in the plays which follow, *Endgame* too has as its prime mover the creative obligation of which its author spoke in *Three Dialogues*. There the nature of the obligation remains obscure ("I don't know" admits Beckett when Duthuit asks him *why* the artist is obliged to create). The insurmountable problem of *statement* which faces Beckett in the essentially theoretical medium of the dialogues is made plain at every turn; indeed it is one reason why these pieces are cast in dialogue-form and not as short essays by Beckett alone—in dialogue he can be meaningfully silent, he can exit weeping, he can even retract his central contentions. But a play like *Endgame* is not confined by the exigencies of theory: it may state (though even then its "statement" will be of a different kind from those made in a theoretical work) but it is not bound to. As we have seen, *Endgame* works by indirection: image, symbol, narrative, gesture and echo all converge patiently on a centre which is, like Hamm himself, unstable, indefinable, perhaps even nonexistent. Ultimately, the play's form constitutes its most significant insight into the essentially ontological nature of the creative obligation.

The Play That Was Rewritten: *Fin de partie*

Ruby Cohn

A play aborted and a play jettisoned contrast with Beckett's favorite play, *Endgame,* which was worked, reworked, and translated from the French. As an approximation, Dierdre Bair is probably right to surmise that Beckett turned to drama when he reached a creative impasse, but drama too can be an impasse, and Beckett labored two years over *Fin de partie.* Of all his plays, it underwent most extensive revision.

Beckett wrote his friend, anglicist Jean-Jacques Mayoux:

> La rédaction définitive de *Fin de partie* est de 56. Mais j'avais abordé ce travail bien avant, peut-être en 54. Une première, puis une deuxième version en deux actes avait précédé celle en un acte que vous connaissez.

> (The final draft of *Endgame* dates from 56. But I had started this work much earlier, perhaps in 54. A first, then a second version in two acts had preceded the one act that you know.)

The "deuxième version en deux actes" of *Fin de partie* is in the Ohio State University Library, and the "première version" is in the Beckett collection of Reading University, England; Beckett does not mention a brief hand-written continuation of the latter, now in Trinity College Library, University of Dublin.

The twenty-one-page typescript at Reading bears no title, but Beckett's hand notes: "avant *Fin de partie.*" Another hand labels the piece "Abandoned

From *Just Play: Beckett's Theater.* © 1980 by Princeton University Press.

Theatre in French,'' and the text does apparently abandon its two actors in the middle of their action. Bair asserts that the play was begun with specific actors in Beckett's mind—Roger Blin who played Pozzo in *Godot* and Jean Martin who played Lucky. If this is so, the new play would continue their roles of master and servant, those staples of French comedy. Designated by the letters X and F (for Factotum), the master's baptismal spoon reads Jeannot, and the servant is variously called Donald, Lucien, and, mainly, Albert. As the letter X suggests, the master is almost as unknowable as Godot, but he is distinctly visible and audible. F wants to address X as "Votre Honneur" or "Monsieur" or even "Patron," but X rejects such honorifics. F declares himself incapable of calling X "vieux con" as directed; nevertheless, he does so once, even while continuing his plea for the privilege of saying: "Votre Honneur."

X and F interact in a place undescribed in the few scenic directions, but Beckett seems to have envisioned a shelter not unlike that of *Endgame,* since F speaks of two large windows (now aveuglées), and he retires to his offstage kitchen, whereas X is confined to his wheelchair. F locates the shelter in Picardy, where destruction occurred "dans des circonstances mystérieuses" between 1914 and 1918. (In the final *Endgame* only Nell's mention of the Sedan hints at the French War, where Napoleon III was disastrously defeated in 1871.) The location may be Picardy, but the props are neutral, and X recites their inventory—a drum and stick attached to X's chair (instead of the later whistle around his neck), a superfluous syringe, a baptismal spoon, and a Bible. X does not mention his Fahrenheit thermometer, but he desires a telescope. Beckett's few scenic directions specify silence, X's drum-beating to summon F, F's entrances and exits, X's vain efforts to move his wheelchair, and F's actual movements of the chair. Beckett evidently heard the dialogue before he saw all the gestures in his mind's eye. And what he heard is an action about playing, passing time, and ending. In X's first expository monologue he says he is blind and paralyzed, then says he is pretending to be blind and paralyzed, then wonders whether he is lying or mistaken. His self-doubt is more insidious than Hamm's, as is appropriate to his name, X. Perhaps the Cartesian heritage is stronger; he doubts, therefore he is, and he doubts out loud.

Of the twenty-one typed pages at Reading University, X's opening monologue (punctuated by ten silences) takes one and a half pages, the first X-F duologue takes four and a half pages, before X recites a shorter monologue. Another five pages of duologue are followed by a shorter X monologue. Like Hamm, X tells a story, and like Hamm he comments on the interaction of master and servant. Unlike *Endgame,* however, this play ends—or breaks off—in duologue (but is carried a little further in the Trinity College manuscript). X addresses F in the *tu* form, but F shows respect for X with his *vous,* instead of the familiar equality of the final version. The pointed pointlessness of the duologues recalls *Godot* and predicts the verbal ping pong of *Endgame:*

> x: Pourquoi ne me tues-tu pas?
> F: (Avec dégoût) Je vous aime. (Silence)
> x: Pourquoi?
> F: Je suis malade.
> x: Moi aussi.
> F: Vous êtes malade?
> x: Je t'aime.
> F: Alors nous nous aimons.

> (x: Why don't you kill me?
> F: [With disgust] I love you. [Silence]
> x: Why?
> F: I'm sick.
> x: Me too.
> F: You're sick?
> x: I love you.
> F: Then we love one another.)

X's story and its enactment—the playing theme—gradually assume importance, but the ending theme of *Endgame* is barely seeded. F repeatedly asks if he may address X as "Your Honor," which privilege is refused. He pleads for the stability of master-servant conventions, and it early becomes evident that this pair, like Vladimir and Estragon before them, have trouble in living through endless time. Dubiously, F remarks that everything has an end, and X retorts with the stale vaudeville joke about the sausage, which has two.

The two men touch on several other subjects that will preoccupy Hamm and Clov—weather, a dog, repetition, F's departure, X's centrality, whether their activities have any meaning. More explicitly than Hamm, X sighs: "Dommage que nous soyons les derniers du genre humain." He requests F to wheel him here and there, to take him for a promenade. The connection between fact and fiction is stronger in the early version: X calls for his dog, then amends this to his wife, and finally shifts to his mother, who becomes the protagonist of his story, as enacted by F.

The mother has had a terrible accident that invalids her, but she is carefully tended: "Et hop la revoilà sur pied (And hup there she is on her feet again)." Three times during his narrative, X cries out disjunctively, "Cherchez-la dans le coin (Look for her in the corner)." After the last time, F enters disguised as the mother, but after a brief mother-son duologue, X instructs F to get rid of that putréfaction. Alone again, X broods: "Nous jouons si mal que ça n'a plus l'air d'un jeu (We're playing so badly that it no longer looks like a game)." Then, resolving that "Cette nuit sera comme les autres nuits (Tonight will be like other nights)" he corrects himself: "Nous ne jouons pas si mal que ça (We're not playing as badly as that)." On his drum X summons F, who informs his master: "Il s'agit de ne pas mourir (It's a question of not dying)." The Reading typescript breaks off after:

> F: Eh bien, il y a toujours l'affaire Bom.
>
> X: Bom. . . . Ah oui, cette pauvre vieille qui réclame une goutte d'eau.
>
> F: Non, ça c'est l'affaire Bim.
>
> (F: Well, there's always the Bom business.
>
> X: Bom. . . . Ah yes, that poor old woman who begs for a drop of water.
>
> F: No, that's the Bim business.)

From the time of his collection of stories *More Pricks Than Kicks,* written over two decades earlier, Bim and Bom recur sporadically in Beckett's work. Russian clowns whose comic routines contained—and were permitted to contain—criticism of the Soviet regime, they became for Beckett emblems of human cruelty, disguised under a comic garb. In a deleted passage of *Godot* Vladimir and Estragon compare Pozzo and Lucky to Bim and Bom. In the Reading University piece Bim and Bom are transformed into parched old women, but, combined with the clown overtones of narration and disguise, their names are a not unfitting terminus for duologues at once cruel and comic.

The Trinity College manuscript continues for two handwritten pages that present a failing X informed by F that an old woman has died of thirst. Less directly reproachful than Clov, F turns a phrase that will later be modified for Hamm:

> X: Et comment sais-tu qu'elle est morte?
> F: Elle ne crie plus.
>
> (X: And how do you know she's dead?
> F: She's no longer crying.)

The Reading University manuscript (and its brief Trinity College continuation) do not manage to weave the several strands: the meditations of X, the master-servant duologues, the X narration that leads to an F enactment. But this abandoned piece already contains *Endgame's* physical space, a climate of illness and disaster, the love-hate interchange of master and servant, their penchant for story and play.

There is no date on the Reading University typescript, so that we cannot know how much time elapsed before Beckett turned to a new version—still untitled but complete by April, 1956—now in Ohio State University Library. We know from Beckett's letter to Jean-Jacques Mayoux that he may have started the first draft as early as 1954, and we know from his letters to Alan Schneider that he began the two-act version in December 1955, so that at least a year separates the two stages.

In the two-act version repetitions underline the playing theme and the ending theme. To some extent Beckett divided the two themes between the two couples who people the play. Master and servant (designated as A and B) are preoccupied with playing out their daily routines. However, the servant is less servile than F, and he is a more versatile player; he appears not only as a woman, but also as a boy. Like the mother of the first draft, this boy is engendered by the master's fiction. The other couple, M and P (for Mémé and Pépé, French for Granny and Grampy) are ending their long lives in stage ashbins. The two main characters, A and B in the manuscript, address each other by Christian names; A is French Guillaume, and B English James. Lacking any other national indication, they both speak colloquial French. M once addresses P as German Walther. A little boy in A's story is French André, but in references to what will become Mother Pegg, Beckett leaves a blank space for a name.

Gone is all reference to Picardy, and the two acts of the Ohio State version take place in the unnational set of the *Endgame* we know, except for the absence of the painting, and the presence of the color red—on Hamm's blanket, robe, nightcap, and handkerchief; on the faces of the three men in act 1. Nell's face is white, in premonition of her death. The "ensign crimson" versus the "pale flag," which Winnie will salvage from *Romeo and Juliet,* are already emblems of life and death. B's beret is yellow and the toy dog black, but other props are nondescript and not described— drum, Bible, and thermometer retained from the earlier draft; new additions are a gaff and an alarm-clock.

When Beckett directed *Endgame* in Berlin in 1967, he segmented the action into sixteen rehearsal scenes, which are already discernible in the two-act version, though differently proportioned. In the final play the ending action dominates the playing action after scene 12, and Beckett emphasizes this in the English translation by borrowing Shakespeare's *Tempest* line, "Our revels now are ended"—in the original French "Finie la rigolade." The French phrase opens act 2 of the earlier draft, appearing on page thirty-five of the sixty-five page typescript.

As in the final *Endgame,* the dialogue of the two-act version begins with an expository soliloquy by Clov-B and ends with a soliloquy of resignation by Hamm-A, but the earlier versions are longer and more repetitive. Clov's opening sentence illustrates the rhythm: "Mort lente, mort rapide, vais-je rester, vais-je le quitter, pour de bon, le quitter pour de bon, ou rester pour de bon, pour la vie, jusqu'à ce qu'il meure, ou jusqu'à ce que moi je meure? (Slow death, rapid death, will I stay, will I leave him, for good, leave him for good, or stay for good, for life, until he dies, or until I myself die?)." However, it is not dialogue but gesture that opens and closes the two-act play, as it does the final *Endgame.* Clov's opening mime is similar to that of *Endgame,* but at play's end Hamm-A buries his face in his hands—a less stoic gesture than curtaining his face with the "old stancher," Beckett's brilliant translation of "vieux linge."

Like his successor Hamm, A simultaneously desires an end and hesitates to end. Although the play in the theater has to end, an endless process is subliminally suggested by the repetition of phrases, gestures, pauses which do not add up to whole events. Of primary importance, therefore, is Beckett's change of Nell-M's death at the end of act 1 to Clov's laconic report in revision: "Looks like it [her death]."

Death *un*happens between the two-act and final *Endgame.* Less decrepit than Nagg, P wants to hold M's hand, and he knocks at the lid of her ashbin. Alarmed that she does not answer, P urges B to examine her bin. The servant bends over, looks in, bends still further. There is a long silence. Then B straightens up, gently covers the bin, and removes his beret. When Nagg-P asks: "Alors?" B removes the old man's skull-cap, but blind A yawns to close the act with French cliché syllables of dismay, "Oh là là."

In act 2 Nell-M's ashbin is gone from the stage. Hamm-A wears a black nightcap, Clov-B a black beret, Nagg-P a black skull-cap. The faces of A, B, and P are white, like M's in act 1; are they close to death? To A's question about whether P is happy that M is dead, the old man replies, "Très." Toward the middle of act 2, P tells B that it isn't worth the trouble to make sawdust for his bin, and B declares that these may be P's last words. They are certainly his last words in this version of the drama. Before the end of the two-act version, A speaks Hamm's final speech of *Endgame* (with a few variants); then he and B engage in a last duologue. B leaves, and A continues to speak a few feeble words. Though A has earlier told B that he has pondered about his last words, the one spoken on stage is simply "Bon."

Present from the beginning of the two-act version is the visual impression of the play we know: two ashbins and one wheelchair in a bare shelter, with two windows that B can reach only by means of a ladder. Although A asks B suspiciously whether he has shrunk (as Hamm will ask Clov), it is rather the dialogue that shrinks between Beckett's two-act and one-act versions (from sixty-five to thirty-seven typed pages). Of the four characters, only Nell-M speaks similar lines although her speeches come in a different order, and she lacks memories of Lake Como.

Beckett curtails many speeches of the three men in the final *Endgame*. Nagg-P no longer comments on Hamm-A's meditations, nor does he declare that Nell-M can crawl out of her bin; nor does he swear an oath on his honor (although Hamm does). Also excised are Clov-B's reminiscences about seaweed and seagulls, his clown business with rolling-pin and telescope, his recitation of an undesignated sonnet, his difficulties with the dative case and pronunciation of the word *Pentateuch,* and his regret that he cannot lie to Hamm-A. From the master Beckett takes away a Pascalian exclamation about infinite spaces, the measurement of temperature at 98.6 Fahrenheit, the recitation of B's basic duties, and A's ruminations about preparing his last words. Excision shortens the A–B duologues where both men struggle through time in sequences about passing the time, about the toy dog, and about tears and laughter. In one routine A and B cry in synchrony, giving a comic tone to their tears. Also deleted is B's hesitation between two commands—that of A to wheel his chair to the center of the shelter and that of P to replace the skull-cap on his head. Both commands desire a return to the *status quo ante,* delaying an end. B weighs his choice: "Mon coeur balance. (*Un temps.*) A moins d'un fait nouveau nous sommes figés pour l'éternité (My heart is poised between the two. (*Pause.*) Unless a new fact enters, we're fixed for eternity)." Eyes front, B begins to recite from Rimbaud: "O saisons, o châteaux!" The impasse passes when A commands that B serve P, and B therefore comments: "On repart. Dommage. (We're off again. Pity)."

Beckett's most telling revision is the complete elimination of two Clov-B scenes of disguise, one in each act. Without the anticlimactic color of these scenes, the ending action becomes more continuous and relentless, apparently dating from the biblical flood. In the two-act draft, the flood reference is specific, for B reads to A from *Genesis,* then turns to the descendants of Shem, chanting a litany of long-lived patriarchs who engendered large families. A's response is Oedipal since he asks for his mother to help him engender. When B protests that A must mean his wife, the master retorts that it's all the same to him whether it is mother, wife, sister, daughter; what counts are two breasts and a vulva. B exits, to reenter in blonde wig, false breasts, and a skirt over his trousers. It is not clear whether A is deceived by the disguise, for B also assumes a woman's voice, and it is B who speaks what will become Nell's line in the final *Endgame*: "Alors, mon gros, c'est pour la bagatelle? (What is it, my pet? Time for love? [Beckett's translation in English *Endgame*])." Since B is both himself and the woman, there follows a comic triangular scene, but instead of two men competing for the favors of the woman, both A and B wish to foist her on the other. If a child is conceived, B's woman's voice tells A, they will drown it.

A child *is* conceived in the two-act draft. Even in the final version, Clov reports seeing a small boy through the window (a report abridged in Beckett's English translation), whereupon Hamm informs Clov that he is no longer needed. In the two-act draft, B surmises this on his own, once the boy is sighted. Soon after A calls his father the boy appears on stage, played by B in his second disguise—red cap, short trousers, and the gray smock of French schoolchildren. Changing voice with costume, B complains of hunger, and A seems to believe B's disguise. He bribes the boy with an offer of chocolate and orders him to look into an ashbin, to push his wheelchair, to bring his gaff. But when B as boy claims the chocolate, A announces that there is no more chocolate. Recalling how he desired a drum when *he* was a child, A offers his instrument to the boy and pleads: "Viens." The boy backs out of the shelter, but blind A continues to address him. He attributes to the boy the greed that Hamm will attribute to old folks. Only after a long silence does A realize that he is alone. He tries vainly to move his chair, as X tried in Beckett's Reading piece, as Hamm will try in *Endgame*. Then, throwing away the gaff, A whispers "Bon," his last word before burying his face in his hands.

In the theater B's disguises would be comic in spite of the grim overtones of Beckett's two-act play. Beckett's elimination of these comic scenes balances his decision to cut the cruellest scene from the earlier draft. In that version P is reluctant to listen to his son's story, so that A orders B to put P's head into a pillory, making him a literally captive audience. A then stages a professor-pupil scene in which he plays both professor and pupil in a lesson on madness. Not satisfied with his father as mere listener, A orders him to recite the story of his life. Changed though he is, P refuses until A, wheeled by B to P's ashbin-pillory hits him on the head with his drumstick, and then threatens him with hammer and gaff. Thus beaten into speech, the old man delivers a seriocomic life story in telegraph phrases. In Beckett's novels Molloy strikes his mother on the head, and a stranger strikes Malone, but Beckett must have decided that such physical violence is too crude for his stage, and Hamm's hostility toward his father is reduced to the verbal in the final *Endgame*. (Servant strikes master with the toy dog in both versions, but the weapon mitigates cruelty.)

In spite of the crucial concentration of two acts into one, the final *Endgame* seems more symmetrical. Hamm and Clov are more evenly balanced than are A and B. Their dialogue is more equitably shared; Clov's five laughs at the beginning are balanced by Hamm's five yawns; Hamm's wheelchair by Clov's ladder; Hamm's dark glasses by Clov's telescope, and his whistle by Clov's alarm clock. Reinforcing such balance is the way Hamm and Clov speak of kissing, whereas Nagg and Nell try to kiss.

Because Beckett's revision achieves balance, economy, and concentration, his few additions are noteworthy. Beckett molded *Endgame* at its beginning and end to suggest that "The end is in the beginning." Thus, only in the final version are all four characters in the same stage space at beginning and end. Only in the finished play does Hamm address his handkerchief as "old stancher" near beginning and end, and only there does he sniff for Clov near beginning and end.

Beckett supplies new binding threads in the final version. He concretizes the difficulties of ending by reference to Eleatic grains and moments, he makes the characters more aware of playing, and he underlines the ending theme by references to more phenomena running out. Dwelling on the entropic action, Beckett embellishes Hamm's wasteland prophecy and his recollection of the painter; Beckett moves the master's richest and loneliest speech to the very end of *Endgame*.

Only into the final version does Beckett introduce the old vaudeville joke about hearing that has not failed—"our what?"—and only there does he add Nagg's significant joke about the poor quality of God's created world. *Endgame* intensifies pathos as well as humor; in the final version alone we find the last moving Hamm-Clov exchange, from Hamm's "Before you go . . . say something" through Clov's most extended speech that begins: "I say to myself—sometimes. . . ." Both characters imply a link between speech and suffering, but that link is stronger in *Endgame* because Beckett's words are stronger, and they are ordered for maximum tension.

The variety of words is diminished by the increase of repetition, which was already markedly increased between the Reading and Ohio State University drafts. Several Clov threats to depart are added to the final version of *Endgame*. The most frequent scenic direction in the Reading fragment is "Silence," but "Un temps" takes the lead in the last two versions, and the final *Endgame* contains new repetitions of "Alors" and "Même jeu." As is often noted, Hamm begins his three soliloquies with the same striking phrase: "A moi de jouer," and in the final version Mother Pegg, the light, and the earth are all "éteint." Repetition itself sounds starker and more continuous in the economy of the single act.

Although the immense effort required to play, pass time, and end is common to the three versions, Beckett did not set out to compose on given themes. He probably began like other playwrights in other styles with characters in a setting—with a paralyzed master and an ailing servant in an almost hermetic room. The two-act version accommodated a second couple. With four characters confined to a single act, however, the play achieves the linear force of a tragedy by Racine, an author long appreciated by Beckett. Still, it is a circle rather than a straight line that diagrams *Endgame,* whose end echoes its beginning, whose hero orders his servant to wheel him *round* his shelter, whose dialogue is riddled by pauses and zeros, in all versions.

Along with sustained themes—playing, passing time, ending—comes a consistency of detail in the three versions. The bare set with its centered wheelchair and off-center ashbins is the dominant image. The physical Bible of the first two drafts evaporates into words in the final version; conversely, the Reading draft merely mentions a dog, which subsequently becomes a visible toy. In the three versions the master accuses the servant of stinking, but the servant's appreciation of the master's honor undergoes a curious development. X's honor, the right to be called "Your Honor," is the most insistent phrase of the Reading draft. In the two-act Ohio State version, honor belongs to Nagg-P, or at least he mentions it when swearing an oath that he will appear when summoned. In the final play it is Hamm who promises on his honor to give Nagg a sugarplum, at which they laugh heartily. The innuendo is that Hamm has no honor, and we learn that he does indeed lack it, for "There are no more sugar-plums"—the only "no more" announced by Hamm rather than Clov. Moreover, the very coupling of honor and sugarplums deflates honor as effectively as does Falstaff.

Few lines of dialogue survive revision into one act. However, each master—in different words—requires his servant to kiss him, and each is refused. In exactly the same words in each version, the master asks the servant why the latter doesn't kill him; in the original French the sound play mitigates the grimness: "Pourquoi ne me tues tu pas?" In another verbal survival through only two versions, Beckett converts a question by

X to a statement by Hamm. The Reading typescript has X anxiously interrogate F: "Est-ce une journée comme les autres jusqu'à présent?" pleading to be reassured about the *in*significance of this day. Early in *Endgame* Hamm asks a comparable question: "C'est une fin de journée comme les autres, n'est-ce pas, Clov?" Hamm is more or less reassured by Clov's reply: "On dirait." Later in *Endgame,* after Hamm tells Clov of the painter's catastrophic vision, master and servant agree that: "Ça a assez duré." And Hamm draws the gloomy conclusion: "Alors c'est une journée comme les autres." The English is more pointedly repetitive: "It's the end of the day like any other day, isn't it, Clov?" and "Then it's a day like any other day."

But of course Hamm is wrong. It is *not* like any other day, for only on this day are there "no more" things, from bicycle-wheels to coffins. Only on this day does Clov sight a small boy and propose to leave. It is only this unending day that Beckett stages, with the symmetries and repetitions that *seem* to support Hamm's conclusion—the old questions, the old answers, the old moves, the old pauses. This day and only this day is distinguished by its brave comic play against a background of tragic waning, but Beckett's skill—exercised in revision—leaves us with Hamm's impression. Hamm is wrong about the insignificance of the day, but he is right to worry about "beginning to mean something." For Beckett has revised *Endgame* into its present meaningful economy.

Endgame: The Playwright
Completes Himself

Sidney Homan

A common practice in the theater is to cover the set once the play is over so that it will be the same set, "virginal" if you will, at the next performance, not changed by the dust and dirt that make their way into the playhouse. *Endgame* opens with the figurative "birth" of its playwright as the servant Clov "*goes to Hamm, removes sheet covering him, folds it over his arms.*" To use the technical term from the Elizabethan stage, Hamm is "discovered," though for a time he is stationary while Clov holds the stage.

Some critics have seen in Clov's opening lines, "Finished, it's nearly finished, it must be nearly finished," echoes of the creation story, though the lines themselves are ambiguous: is the creation (Hamm?) nearly finished and therefore soon to blossom in its own right? Or is the world about to end, "finished?" Clov then departs for the kitchen, his own orderly offstage world ("Nice dimensions, nice proportions").

On Clov's departure, Hamm himself completes the discovery, first yawning under the handkerchief that covers his head and then removing it to reveal a "*Very red face. Black glasses.*" Hamm's opening line, "Me," may suggest a tremendous ego, though, as we will see, an ego quite appropriate if we think of him as the play's lead actor, its ham or Hamlet, or perhaps the playwright himself, the creative force behind the stage world. A second yawn introduces the next suggestive line, actually a continuation of "Me": "to play." We might take the word *play* either as a verb—meaning "now I will play"—or as a noun, a compression of "to the play": Hamm will

From *Beckett's Theaters: Interpretations for Performance.* © 1984 by Associated University Presses, Inc.

now get to his play. We have heard the phrase before in Beckett: Malone speaks of "play" and the *Unnamable* directs "Worm to play." If, to echo Hamm himself, we would allow "every man his speciality," then I believe that Hamm's *speciality* is creation itself, however bleak the created world of this play may seem.

I

Hamm's creation here seems to be an internal one, that inner world peopled by the imagination of a blind man. Whereas Clov is concerned with the external, with the one physical setting itself—he speculates that "There's nowhere else"—Hamm's concern is that of "Text 2": "Perhaps we're in a head." Deprived of a sense of perspective by his blindness, he can only think of man and, more specifically, of himself as the macrocosm. Appropriately, his speculation is that there is "no one else." For Hamm the external world *is* the illusion, in the most negative sense of that word: "Outside of here it's death."

At the start Hamm is asleep, his power of creation dormant. He may well be dreaming, for several times during the play he makes reference to the pleasures of this state. As in the medieval dream vision, he moves, after Clov's discovery, from sleep to waking, from dreams to the *informing* of his dreams. The source of that informing, as it was for the medievalist, is not ultimately the external world, for the vision, thus formed, is only an approximation of an internal state that, without art, cannot be known.

There is a falling off, a loss of clarity as one moves from the dream vision to the waking reality. If Hamm could continue sleeping he "might make love"; he might "go into the woods . . . and [his] eyes would see . . . the sky, the earth." His vision here is one of absolute freedom, of a world where one can move, "run"—ironic for an invalid confined to a wheelchair. Still, this idyllic world conjured by the dreamer's fancy is irrelevant to the present play, whose concern, as Hamm immediately qualifies the vision, is the "Nature" of his own "head" and "heart." If that idyllic world, where one is free in space and time, *is* reality, it represents an external force that, later made manifest in the figure of the small boy, would intrude on and ultimately destroy the artist's fictive inscape.

This inner space, the single stage set before us, is the artist's domain, the "now" informed by the narrative itself, with a past that is either irrelevant or tragic (sometime in the past Nagg and Nell lost their legs) and a future that is either irrelevant or potentially tragic (the boy who threatens to unravel Hamm's creation). In an extraordinary compression of the body's two most vital organs, Hamm finds his "heart in his head" (the line is repeated by Nagg), thereby reversing the cliché about thinking with one's heart. The playwright's internal process is a rational one: the feelings of the heart, those emotions allowing him to react positively or negatively to life, are given form in the head. By a sort of reverse gravity the juices of the heart flow upward to the head; Hamm confesses that there is something "dripping" in his head.

We have made a quantum leap from *Godot*. There the set, while clearly external, was sparsely populated, and so the impoverished tree and rock only underscored the barren outer world that, given the intellectual and imaginative capacities of Vladimir and Estragon, served as an appropriate stage for their waiting. Here the set is an inner one, a room, but it is heavily populated with ashbins, a ladder, windows, a picture, numerous props, and with the suggestion of a kitchen just offstage. However, this relatively lavish set, if taken literally, seems an inadequate correlative for the world Hamm struggles to define. Clov, who dons a traveler's costume in the play's final moments, may be a holdover from *Godot*. If this is so, then Hamm, while not Godot himself, is a dominant force, a master or godlike figure who, more than the relatively shallow Pozzo, might be a suitable object for the tramps' quest in the earlier play.

Hamm is physically blind, and Clov must serve as his eyes. Still, the inner eye, the "mind's eye" (1.2.185) as Hamlet would have it, works overtime here. That eye sees not objective reality, nor is it subject to the historic materialism that confirmed existence for those eighteenth-century philosophers like Berkeley whom Beckett studied and in part rejected. Instead, Hamm's "eye" views only an "infinite emptiness" that is "all around." The trick in *Endgame* is to "play" on that infinite emptiness, to give it form through words, even though words themselves are ultimately only empty abstractions. The "game," in the sense that word is used in "Enueg I," is to make something—however meager—out of nothing. Hamm's prediction is that Clov will someday experience that same emptiness, seeing, like the painter-engraver, the apparent something of the external world for what it truly is.

That engraver, surely, is a surrogate for the central character, because Hamm has no other source of reference than himself and yet finds it too painful, as well as inappropriate by the rules of this endgame, to reveal himself too completely too soon. For the engraver the entire physical world, from rising corn to the sails of the herring fleet, all that "loveliness" as bounded by land and sea, was nothing—"ashes." Even the possibility of an external world subject to the engraver's or—as Hamm alters it—painter's interpretation no longer exists, for that was "way back," during a time "in the land of the living." Clov delivers the benediction to a reality that is no more: "God be with the days." When he complains that today, in contrast, "There are so many terrible things," he errs not so much in the adjective "terrible" as he does in the assumption that there are still "things." Hamm cautiously corrects him: "No, no, there are not so many now." That correction allows for the more proper definition of the present world, a world of theater or play, an artifice created by Hamm: "Do you not think this has gone on long enough?" It is the play world, then, that is "this . . . this . . . thing." Hamm doubts that Clov will be equal to the task of giving form to nothing or this inner world of artifice, doubting that his actor can turn playwright. (As we shall see, the play itself, *Endgame,* partially disproves this gloomy assessment, but then Hamm has an image to protect.)

Hamm's play thereby becomes the informing of his "misery"—of himself, to be more exact. Whereas Clov has "nothing to say," Hamm has a "few words" to "ponder" in his heart, the heart that, we know, leads to the head. For him the greater his suffering the "emptier" he must become: the resulting form has an inverse correlation to its origin. Lesser men—if we can stand Hamm's arrogant pronouncement at the opening of the play— can hold a greater portion of their suffering. Hamm's lot, the playwright's lot—and the very condition about which Shakespeare complains in his Sonnets—is to express everything, to prostitute inner emotions before an audience. The artistic fate is analogous, as several contemporary artists have observed, to the act of masturbation, a metaphor Beckett will revisit in *Eh Joe.* It must be complete, not half-hearted; and once started, there is no turning back. The act is intimate and pleasurable—yet sterile in any biological sense. Hence the bleak bomb shelter of Hamm's world is also the hive of great imaginative activity. Once this inner world is "peopled," given form, the tragedy itself is not resolved but rather is made public. The tragedy remains gruesome, yet there is an aesthetic pleasure in the form, and hence we applaud, rather than weep, at its conclusion. This informing is essentially comic, and while parents may die in Beckett's plays and novels (in *Malone Dies,* for example), the lead characters do not. In Beckett the lead characters' informing of their tragedies, whether it be Malone on his deathbed or Winnie in her earthly prison, depends on their own consciousness of their creation. Malone has a pad and a pencil, however much they have deteriorated; and Winnie has props galore, plus half-remembered snatches from songs, proverbs and poetry. Aesthetic "life" springs from thematic "death," and in *Endgame* death, though ever-present, does not touch Hamm. Similarly, Vladimir and Estragon, though only dim creators when compared with Hamm, cannot die: the suicide tree is inadequate and the belt breaks.

As a creator Hamm craves rain, since its nourishment is necessary for the seeds of his mind; Clov is equally positive that it won't rain. Eager for Clov's seeds to sprout, Hamm is distressed when Clov contends that they won't. He then suggests that Clov might do well to scratch about a bit more; perhaps they were planted too early.

If Hamm opens the play by enumerating his miseries, it is still true that he, as opposed to Nagg whom he dismisses as an "accursed progenitor," is the blessed progenitor of *Endgame* and is strangely optimistic, despite those miseries, whereas Clov, the son, is the pessimist. Old-fashioned in such optimism, Hamm is the sometimes benevolent god or the playwright as god to his little world. Positioned at its center, given to surveying the walls defining its circumference, attended by his not always obedient Ariel—who, like his Shakespearean prototype, also yearns for freedom—Hamm is a jealous god, fearful of having any other god raised before him, whether it be in the person of a small boy or a flea. Like Prospero, he is a word-giver, both father and teacher to Clov. And he is egocentric, as gods are wont to be, just as Vladimir and Estragon are ego-deficient, as true subjects are wont to be. The single set of *Endgame*, the shabby room, *is* the world, the theater of the world both literal and figurative that the father, the playwright, offers his adopted son, Clov. "You can't leave us," he explains ruthlessly, for Clov is an inseparable part of Hamm's world.

Again, Kenner's hypothesis, that the set of *Endgame* resembles the inside of a human skull, with the two rear windows serving as eyes, is especially relevant here. For when the generation of the 1970s spoke of "blowing the mind," that phrase only implied a readjustment in the mind's link to external reality. But "outside of here," outside *Endgame*'s set, outside the mind that is being informed through the artistic process, it is clearly "death." Life, in Beckett's definition here, is not a fact but rather a process involving conscious creation through words, and also actions, as in the two mimes. By such creation one gives the "illusion" of existence, a conscious artifice to be set against the misguided assumption of reality held by those outside *Endgame*'s single stage set. I think it is his avoidance of death, of nothingness, an avoidance not studied but inevitable, that makes Beckett, like Shaw's hero in *Arms and the Man*, the "true romantic."

Hamm as god, Hamm as artist—the ascription seems to work both ways. If he is a god, his world is horribly shrunken, yet, however shrunken that world, Hamm guards it jealously against the rival, outside world of earth, water, color, and light that he knows only through his servant's reports. Omniscient on the stage set, his knowledge of this outside "set" is fully dependent on Clov's eyes. In the several drafts of *Endgame*, Beckett pared away at the description of that rival world, particularly as embodied in the young boy. Yet the mere suggestion of its existence terrifies Hamm, even though for us, as audience, the poverty of reality only accents the richness of the ever-present "little room" before us.

Conversely, we may see Hamm as the artist, his world limitless, eternally growing in his head and heart. Waiting for the painkiller may be only a comic bow in the direction of *Godot*. In point of fact, Hamm as artist uses words as productively in informing his suffering as Vladimir and Estragon used words unproductively in waiting for what they imagine will be their savior, rather than their painkiller or terminus.

Given to stories, Hamm is his own story and storyteller, the narrator/narrated, spinning his tales spiderlike from within himself. Beckett's artists, such as Words in *Words and Music,* protest that the stories do not come from inside them, but I think that by such assertions they only call attention to the ultimate end, the informing or "publication" of an inner vision. All begins from within, from "Me" (again, Hamm's first word), from precisely that acute consciousness that Clov for the most part lacks and that Vladimir and Estragon experience only in dream lapses, or when Lucky and Pozzo provide a mirror image of their own condition. As we shall see, the story of the man begging alms for his son is only superficially about someone else. As Hamm says, "There's no one else," and in his way Hamm embodies all people: he is the man seeking bread, and the object of that charity, and the stern judge who denies succor, and Mother Pegg who, like Socrates, seeks truth with her light, as well as Mother Pegg barely existing in her final days with that light extinguished. In a sense the play is one large monologue parading as a four-character drama. Like Shakespeare's Richard II in his cell, Hamm peoples his little world through this union of heart and head—his equivalent for that coupling of mind and soul in his royal counterpart.

Thus constricted, Hamm sets about creating, or "we do what we can"; it is "slow" and, I would add, painful "work." For that story actors are required—and hence Clov. The playwright also needs an audience; unlike the theoretical audience for those novels with which Beckett began his career, the audience here is actual. So dependent, the artist's inner vision relies for its informing on the collective abilities and consciousness of a host of people. The play is a public testament to an inner world. Krapp's one book was a failure—*Effie* sold only thirteen copies—whereas his tape recordings are overheard by a real audience.

If such publication of an inner state can "mean something," then perhaps it "won't all have been for nothing." Given this pragmatic, even didactic sense of mission, I find it misguided, though natural, to say that Beckett has nothing to say. Hamm's struggle to make or to mean something, "to say" himself—to borrow a favorite infinitive from Beckett—separates him as playwright light years from writers of the so-called absurdist theater.

II

Clov is the actor to Hamm's playwright, and the latter rightly observes that "gone from me you'd be dead." Conversely, Hamm needs Clov or, as at the end, must turn actor himself to preserve the play. If Vladimir and Estragon are halves of a common personality—brains and body, head and feet, speaker and doer—then so are Hamm and Clov, with an added aesthetic dimension. Clov can't sit: he acts, in the broadest sense of that word. And Hamm can't do anything but sit. He is the cerebral half, both in terms of life and the theater. The literal food, the carrots and radishes that Vladimir furnished Estragon, are here symbolic food: the words, the dialogue. It is to this linguistic food that Hamm refers, I believe, when he threatens to give Clov "nothing more to eat." Clov's "Then we'll die" sustains the theme of a joint aesthetic life. If the actor goes, the playwright's mouthpiece goes, and hence the playwright is rendered inoperative. Some compromise is needed; as "Text 1" phrases it, "let them [the body and the head or, if you will, Clov and Hamm] work it out between them." So Hamm continues, "I'll give you just enough to keep you from dying. You'll be hungry all the time." Surely we have here a perfect description of the increasingly sparse dialogue characterizing Beckett's plays. The lips are both the initial "confrontation" for food destined for the body and—as Ionesco describes so graphically in *The Lesson*—the final outpost for words on their way out into the public atmosphere of conversation or stage dialogue.

In this way the physical relationship between the two always has an aesthetic "otherside." Hamm is concerned whether or not he has made Clov suffer too much or too little; when Clov replies that he hasn't been forced to suffer unduly, Hamm is ecstatic. By Hamm's own admission in that first speech, his concern is presenting his own misery—read "tragedy." The more of that tragedy Clov as actor can undertake, the more complete will be Hamm's expression of his inner nature. Like his Shakespearean namesake, Hamm is concerned with the golden mean of expression. Too little suffering, and hence too little to be experienced by the audience, and the play fails to mean enough. Too much suffering to express, and the actor might die onstage. Either way threatens to abort the process. One must fit action to the word, the word to the action.

As with the Unnamable, others' sufferings are "nothing compared" to those of the artist. Yet others, however deficient in the experience of tragedy, must embody the artist's supreme suffering, whether it be in the form of the Unnamable's fictive characters or Hamm's not-completely-pliant actor. In this sense, Winnie is as much actor as artist; properly, she is surrounded by the artifacts of other artists, whether it be the advertising copy on the toothbrush or actual lines from Shakespeare and Browning. The ultimate artist is absent in *Godot,* though, as I have argued, the tramps try their hand at creation in the second act, even if it be an art that passes the time and does little else. Once Hamm has emerged as artist, even as Beckett feels his way in what was still, for him, a relatively new medium, artists will come at us galore: Krapp, Henry, plus assorted Openers, and Voices, and Mouths. The issue in *Endgame* is how to sustain the tragedy until the fruit ripens sufficiently for the final scene. Die too early or die too late—these are the grounds for melodrama, not tragedy.

Though Hamm and Clov complement each other, their relationship is still an uneasy one, and as the play progresses the disciple threatens revolt. Like Shakespeare's Caliban, he would cease to be only a "brute beast." At one point Clov even hurls the dog—the symbol of Hamm's sterile, albeit illusory creation—at his master. But then Beckett's couples always fight; the halves of the composite soul, like the warring body and soul in count-less Renaissance poems, are necessary, inevitable, but unhappy bedfellows. Vladimir and Estragon are continually threatening separation; Willie, whom Winnie needs as audience, promises either love or murder at the end of *Happy Days*; Molloy and Moran may ultimately be the same being, but the latter seeks to capture the former; the head in *The Unnamable* depends on a waitress who is also a torturer; and for the narrator of *How It Is* to speak with Pim he must deliver an anal insult ("stab him simply in the arse that is to speak") to his counterpart before the dialogue can begin.

This division is inseparable from the complementary qualities. Clov *must* war with Hamm, actor with playwright, because Clov, constitution-ally unlike the playwright, can assert his integrity only as a reverse image of his master's. Truman Capote once spoke of actors as being dumb crea-tures who only mouth the dialogue as directed. Hamlet himself fears that the clowns of the visiting troupe will ignore the lines of that playwright ultimately responsible for *The Murder of Gonzago*. Playwrights, however, speak from personal bias and, important as they are, are not fully responsible for what happens on stage.

Accordingly, Clov, when compared with the hyperimaginative Hamm, is more a creature of "habits," therefore siding with that half of the habit/imagination dichotomy established by Beckett in his book on Proust. Imagination is the road leading to tragedy, and Hamm fully assumes the tragic post of the sufferer at the end. Habit keeps the specter of tragedy distant, and Clov at the end reappears backstage, away from Hamm's tragic center, dressed like some vaudeville comedian: "*Enter Clov, dressed for the road. Panama hat, tweed coat, raincoat over his arm, umbrella, bag.*" In place of Hamm's large and often spectacular mental "visions" (Flora, Pomona, a new mental world that replaces the present stinking universe, the ocean, the waves, the horizon, the sun), Clov sees only "gray." His real focus is not on the mind but on the audience surrounding the stage. Whereas Hamm, until his last speech, is primarily responsible for his personal visions, Clov as actor gives first priority to us. He sees in his glass "a multitude . . . in transports . . . of joy."

When it comes time for Clov's one original idea, the limits of his mental abilities are clearly contrasted with Hamm's own "prolonged creative effort." Clov decides to set his alarm clock so that if Hamm whistles for him and he fails to come, then it will follow that even though the alarm rings, he is gone. If the alarm doesn't ring, then he is dead. Hamm then proceeds to destroy Clov's logic with the suggestion that the alarm might not work because it is used either too much or too little. The disciple, in his own immediate and highly physical way, then argues with the master by bringing in the alarm clock and letting it chime against Hamm's ear. Clov's practical demonstrations, though, fail to override the fact that the idea of using an alarm to determine spatial presence or absence is a poor one. Hamm's cynicism about Clov's intelligence remains: "This is perhaps not one of my bright days, but frankly—." A direction-taker, not a direction-giver, a deliverer not a visionary, Clov clings for most of the play to habit and its corollary order. The object of his intellection, the alarm clock, betrays the poverty of his own vision, of a mechanistic universe ruled by time, where existence or absence is measured by the sound or nonsound from a mechanical contrivance, this in a play otherwise mocking mechanisms (the dog with three legs) or destroying them (the bicycles). Instead of the imaginative space of Hamm's stage, Clov prefers his own kitchen with its "nice dimensions, nice proportions," for there he can "lean on the table, and look at the wall, and wait for him to whistle me." The irony here is that the realistic, well-ordered kitchen is never seen, while the surrealistic stage, with its implications as an allegory for Hamm's inner life, is all that we have as audience. Clov's place of order and logic is therefore,

at very least, as illusory as anything else in the play. His is a space-and-
time-bound world, one having little room for process, uncertainties, let
alone the imagination. He likes beginnings and endings, the clear extremes
of an otherwise often incoherent existence: for him the "end is terrific,"
whereas Hamm prefers the "middle." At one point Clov would "stop
playing"; Hamm, on the other hand, must always be playing, must always
be part of an imaginative evolution.

Even this dichotomy breaks down. In section v we shall see how at
the end Hamm, in Clov's absence, must become actor as well as playwright.
(If Hamm and Clov are, in fact, halves of one composite soul, then Hamm
has been this actor all along.) In a parallel fashion, Clov rises above the
level of a trained puppet as the play itself "gets" to the actor, even as the
play "gets" to the audience.

In his last speech—indeed, a speech that is an exception to his usual
short lines—Clov becomes positively creative. He responds to Hamm's
direction to "articulate," to say "a few words . . . from [his] heart." He
talks first of the disparity between a theological promise and the reality that
he knows. His most imaginative line, that last line with its picture of "they"
who are "dying of their wounds," offends Hamm. Clov has overstepped
the bounds between actor and playwright, and is promptly silenced by
Hamm with a short "Enough!" His insight is too piercing; the servant, like
Words and Music, revolts from the master and threatens to run off with
the play. This violation of the actor's lower estate threatens Hamm's cen-
tralist position. Still Clov continues:

> I say to myself—sometimes, Clov, you must learn to suffer
> better than that if you want them to weary of punishing you—
> one day. I say to myself—sometimes, Clov, you must be there
> better than that if you want them to let you go—one day. But
> I feel too old, and too far, to form new habits. Good, it'll never
> end, I'll never go.
> (*Pause.*)
> Then one day, suddenly, it ends, it changes. I don't understand,
> it dies, or it's me, I don't understand, that either. I ask the words
> that remain—sleeping, waking, morning, evening. They have
> nothing to say.
> (*Pause.*)
> I open the door of the cell and go. I am so bowed I only see my
> feet, if I open my eyes, and between my legs a little trail of black
> dust. I say to myself that the earth is extinguished, though I
> never saw it lit.

> (*Pause.*)
> It's easy going.
> (*Pause.*)
> When I fall I'll weep for happiness.

He dares to use one of Hamm's words, "suffer," and he now realizes that there is a limit to "habits," since they can only gloss over the deeper, more terrifying realities of our existence. Now the words flow from Clov's playwright's lips: "sleeping, waking, morning, evening." He knows that words are nothing, "have nothing to say," and in saying that he himself gives form to the nothingness, the very artistic process defined in my closing comments on *Waiting for Godot*. At last a metaphor worthy of a Pozzo or a Vladimir—or a Godot. Life becomes "a little trail of dust," and the speech ends, all passions spent, with a diminuendo of two short phrases: "It's easy going" and "When I fall I'll weep for happiness."

Clov's character, somewhat like Gloucester's in *King Lear,* has at last approached that of the central character. For Gloucester moves from a shallow courtier to a concerned patriot to a man suffering physical insult, all of which acts as the subplot correlative for Lear's mental anguish. Gloucester's "renaissance," even as it moves him closer to the original pattern set by the greater, betrayed father figure, also demands his extinction as a character. Similarly, Clov, a "mere" actor given to symmetry and habit and to following directions, now experiences his own little "renaissance." At his own endgame, even if it be merely leaving the stage rather than life, he waxes poetic and is, despite a surly disposition, clearly imaginative. He turns playwright, momentarily fusing his character with Hamm's. Then *"Exit Clov"* before he can do the last favor of covering Hamm with a sheet.

The alienation between Hamm and Clov, master and slave, king and fool, if you will, has been mitigated for a few moments. The charade of dualism has been momentarily exposed, for the signification of dramatic language is a joint venture of playwright and actor: the writing is not distinct from the saying. In his moment of poetic inspiration, with the ironic dialectic of its negative theme, Clov carries Hamm's monologue toward dialogue and then back toward the brief monologue of one who will remain outside the final "play" of Hamm's tragic ascension. As if to signify metadramatically this aborted but parallel renaissance in himself, Clov refers to the actual condition of the play: "This is what we call making an exit." He sees the play as a creator, if only for a moment; but, no less important, he sees the play now as the creator himself sees it. A few social graces exchanged between master and servant let us down from this veritable

Pyrenees of the muse, and then, with the Clov character complete—having run the gamut from actor to audience to playwright and now back to one whose last two actions will be covering Hamm with the sheet and, this done, making an exit—the character, as a speaking character that is, disappears, represented only by the physical shell of his former verbal-physical self. We have seen or shall see such shells elsewhere in Beckett: the silent Lucky, Krapp staring motionless at us in the final moments of his play, Joe, Keaton at the end of *Film,* the garbage in *Breath,* the silent responder in *Not I,* and so on. The play now reverts to its beginning, as Hamm repeats his opening line of "Me to play." What Hamm does will be the subject of a later section; for now, as prelude to that final ascent of the hero, we examine the other characters, Nagg and Nell, and the little boy, who is beyond both dialogue and tableaux.

III

In one sense Nagg and Nell represent a horrible extension of Clov's unimaginative mentality. Their demands are not for the food of a playwright, but for their own "pap"; indeed, one of Nagg's first lines is "Me pap!" If Beckett's theater, as I have argued in the *Godot* chapter, thrives on the aesthetics of that present established by actor and audience, then the parents are nothing more than creatures of pressing and present physical desire: to eat, to be scratched, to make love as best they can in the ashbins.

Conversely, they are mired in the past, imaginatively and mentally. In this sense, if Hamm represents the theatrical present, Clov the impossible future (he expends great effort in getting out of his current prison), then Nagg and Nell are Beckett's vision of some perverse Wordsworthian emotion recollected in tranquillity. They speak of adventures in the Ardennes, the road to Sedan, and later of Lake Como. The bicycle, so often Beckett's symbol of would-be freedom, has also led to the accident that cost both of them their legs. The visions of loving, traveling, rowing on the lake, and getting into such "fits" (sexual?) that the boat capsized—all is past. Such resurrected memories are clearly voluntary, mechanical, and trite, part of a habitual pattern to efface the present. Conversely, when their son, Hamm, tries to imagine parallel adventures—a trip to the South, adrift on a raft, carried far away—he is abruptly pulled back to the present, the projected trip canceled amidst neurotic speculations about the dangers of sharks. Past and future seem only theoretical possibilities; the present—in *Godot,* the present waiting—is all Beckett's characters have. The issue appears to be the quality of that existence lived only in the present. On this score Nagg and Nell are even more crippled than their son. Their own adventures capsizing on Lake Como will recall Krapp's one meaningful experience with the lady in the rowboat. However, that moment for Krapp signaled the end of a love affair, and Krapp, as I will suggest in a later chapter, is able to capitalize, as Hamm's parents cannot, on that memory when he frantically tries a fresh recording to link his present state with memories of his youth.

If Hamm moves toward an imaginative reconstruction of some inner reality, for the parents the present is nothing more than a "farce." Their sight, both physical and artistic (visionary), is going; even the sand in the bottom of their ashbins is not the procreative seashore sand of *Cascando*, but only a cheap substitute for the much-preferred sawdust. Despite many arguments, Hamm in his concern for Clov provides his own "son" with the materials for acting and does so, as we have seen, in the moment just before Clov's exit, where the disciple comes into his own as an artist. In contrast, Nagg—"nagging," even as the name Nell suggests, among other things, death's "knell"—has lost his son, both by his anger at Hamm's ingratitude and by Hamm's own incompatibility with an unimaginative old man. In this way Nagg and Nell represent a play within the play, the countermovement to what I take as the procreative, romantic relationship (however strained) between Hamm and Clov and—at length—the audience. Nagg and Nell are a couple, one of the few in Beckett, who do "die" as stage characters with dialogue, who have lost even more than their mobility. Hamm has lost his, to be sure, but that loss is only a springboard to the cultivation of an inner vision. Their movement, however, is a constrictive one from a vaguely romantic past, to tales unwanted and unappreciated by Nagg, to a craving for physical comforts that only mocks their imprisonment, to silence, and at length extinction.

The father's seeking food for the son may bear analogy to Hamm's providing theatrical dialogue for Clov; and the mother Pegg's seeking light may at length suggest the inner visions of the central character. Even the tailor, whose product, he boasts, is finer than God's created world, stands as a parody of Hamm's product, the informing of his vision that resists the other creative world, that of the small boy threatening from the outside. Yet Nagg and Nell contradict Hamm's achievement, for the food they want is literally biscuits—and they are fussy as to the brand—and later sugarplums. Clov is also unimaginative for most of the play in his obsession with "putting things in order" and clearing "everything away," but at least this constitutes his "dream," albeit an excessively mechanical, even sterile one when compared with Hamm's own dreams of magical forests. Nagg's and Nell's light, in contrast, is literally extinguished each time Clov is told to "Screw down the lids." Nagg's own "product" is a dirty joke, an anecdote, but hardly the "prolonged creative effort" of his son.

Some critics see the silence achieved by Nagg and Nell as Beckett's own wished-for goal, a cessation of the tension between habit and imagination, between the desire to stop and the enervating desire to go on. Thus Nell's line is taken as a momentary vision of a paradise that Beckett rarely grants his characters: "It was deep, deep. And you could see down to the bottom. So white. So clean." Still, Nell's death wish is contrary, I would think, to the painful, inevitable, but creative tension elsewhere in the play. Beckett's dramas—all of them—are about generating motion from meager sources, about—this is the bottom line—going on, about not sinking.

If hers is a genuine vision of the ablation of desire and of the comfort of total silence, of a formless world, like that in "Enough," where the quintessence of noncolor coincides with the quintessence of nonsound, then Nell still cannot inform the present with that vision. It remains only a voluntary memory of happier days, eternally confined by the past tense "was," ironically contradicted by the present, in which Lake Como has degenerated to a dry ashbin. Only by truly involuntary memory can one achieve endless mobility in the third region of darkness, so dark, so unconnected to the external world that darkness is paradoxically the same as infinite light and whiteness. Even in "Enough" memory turns sour as the lover describes a serene union with the master that is no more. For all Beckett's yearning for silence, that yearning, when expressed through characters, is either no less futile (Henry in *Embers* may pass into silence in the Bolton-Holloway story, but the concluding sound of the sea mocks his achievement) or is hideously parodied as in the present case. Instead of achieving formlessness, the parents are encased in absurdly rigid forms, just as their silence is conveyed either as a past no longer probable or as a condition imposed on them by a frustrated Godot, by their son who ironically commits theatrical "parricide" to silence them.

Hamm's parallel in *Eh Joe* is down on his luck, to say the least, berated by the off-camera voice, possibly reduced to solitary masturbation. Still, the voice may be an inner one, and Joe may, like Hamm, be giving voice to his inner suffering: conscience, to misquote Hamlet, doth make artists of us all. In trying to pass the time for themselves, Vladimir and Estragon also pass the time for us. Try as they may, they cannot die. Even if we reduce the years between birth and death to silence, or to the rubbish strewn horizontally on the stage, the death cry in *Breath* is still indistinguishable from the birth cry, from the "vagitus," as it is called, that opens that play. "I can't go on, I'll go on." Such affirmative voices are missing in Nell's terrifying vision of a downward spiral into white noise, sterile sand, and a silence that would deny the very words that are our one hold on being.

Nagg curiously needs Nell as audience for his stories, though she protests the role. If we think of their forming with us the other half of a theater-in-the-round, then Nagg and Nell are our own reverse images. Like us they are confined to seats, a captive audience, even if that comparison is a bit bizarre. However, in moving from a potentially significant, surely happier past to their own isolated, present physical wants, they may at length alienate us. For surely we watch *Endgame,* this narrative nicely embodying the three unities and centering on the tragic informing and therefore realization of its central character, because the play itself treats, however obliquely, issues above those of physical appetite. It takes a strong purpose, a reading above the epicurean, to "stomach" *Endgame.* Our audience surrogates on stage have copped out in favor of Sprat's Medium and sugarplums, and ambiguous orders for back scratches. Nor do they stay to the end as viable links between stage and audience.

As the parents retreat into themselves, figuratively as well as literally, Clov and Hamm increasingly move out toward us. Clov does this by definition, as an actor warming to his role. Even Hamm, though at first the isolated, self-pitying playwright confined like Marlowe's Faustus to his study, will become at the end both supreme playwright and actor, feeding himself the very dialogue (or monologue) that he has written.

IV

Hamm's emergence, however, is inseparable from the play's own complex, indeed divided attitude toward art and the imagination. His final performance—and it is toward this performance that the present analysis moves—is, I think, not so much comic or tragic—though some critics see the play itself as a tragicomedy—as it is "inevitable" in Aristotle's sense: the complex final performance mirroring an ongoing, equally complex attitude toward art, here defined as a collaboration of playwright and actor (and ratified by the audience).

Again, this emergence of the playwright-actor occurs in a theater of the mind. Beckett's stage is small because our landscape itself has withered, or never was. If the microcosm of the stage reflects the macrocosm of the "real" (in Beckett's sense) world offstage, then it is right that when Clov looks out he sees this very same diminished world: no sails, no fins, no smoke, but only a light that is "sunk," no gulls, nothing on the horizon, only leaden waves, a "zero" sun, neither light nor day but only gray, "GRRAY!" Perhaps this is akin to the "grey incandescence" of which Malone speaks. Here is material, in Clov's mind, for a "farce"—but nothing beyond that.

Only in the radio plays do we have a change of scenery: the road and the station in *All That Fall,* the journey toward the sea in *Cascando.* In these works the scenery, because it has no physical correlative, is surely an interior one. *Film* concerns precisely the abandonment of larger vistas (the street, even the stairway) for the final end, the room/womb of the mind. A later play, *Not I,* gives up the pretense of a recognizable set, reducing the stage to a man and a mouth, to man and his female conscience, or man-audience and mouth-actor. The itinerary of *Murphy* or *Molloy* and the Irish ramblings of *More Pricks Than Kicks* are as much a thing of Beckett's past as is his addiction to Joyce. If "nature" means the country or landscape, then there is "no more nature" in *Endgame,* at least not in the "vicinity." The doctor himself, perhaps the god of the created world, is dead. The issue now is not man in relation to nature or environment or society, but man in relation to his soul-sole self, to that society, always within us, which we may deny or defraud by the busy work of habit, and yet the society that at death— recall the saying that everyone must die alone—is our only refuge.

If all of this suggests a diminished arena for art, and for the artist, Hamm observes that it is still better than nothing. He would reject the realist's elevation of environment—be it Hardy or Dreiser or Skinner—as a dominant factor and hence the proper subject matter for art. Properly, Beckett celebrates a subjective and therefore impressionistic art. The outer, as Hamm says, is hell. If the rejection of the external world is painful, if we hesitate in taking the inward journey into the informing of our own suffering and aloneness, Hamm's reassurance is that there are not so many terrible things as we imagined. I. A. Richards echoes the sentiment when he argues that the avoidance of fear constitutes the tragedy; properly, fear is a process, not an object (*Principles of Literary Criticism*).

Clov's practical, cynical question, "What is there to keep me here?," is met by Hamm's straightforward "The dialogue." When Polonius asks Hamlet what he is reading, the Prince's reply, "Words, words, words" (2.2.193), may indeed be cynical on the surface: what else does one read? Or it may mean: all that I have is words. I take the response, however, as a celebration of the theater that is, ultimately, words; and in the world of Denmark, one of deception, of lustful addiction to objects, in that world elevating physical achievement, even activity above introspection and intellection, language and those arts associated with it *are* a precious commodity. Clov sees Hamm's "story" as only a "farce, day after day," the very word used by Nagg; but both confuse limited stories—the anecdotes, the recollections—with a larger story, the entire process of *Endgame* that encircles them and gives them meaning, even if that meaning implies that situation here is artificial, this union of playwright and actor and audience still denies, through the use of words, that horrible reality in which each of us is alone, most certainly alone in death as our personal endgame approaches.

As the play moves toward the complex portrait of art and of the playwright-actor who conceives of and then delivers that art, Hamm's own sense of the theater, always keen of course, accelerates. Increasingly, he is given to theatrical terms, sharing an inside joke with us even as he draws closer to the offstage audience and away from the mock audience in ashbins behind him. He seems to acknowledge our presence while we, as audience, ratify his story by our being there. Accordingly, he speaks of his "soliloquy" and of an "underplot." Clov himself talks of making an "exit." We thereby may have before us really two stories, or three, if you will: a main plot, that of Hamm and Clov, in which the inner "stage" comes to the surface; a minor plot, that of Nagg and Nell, where the stage shrinks and is at length extinguished; and, as Hamm himself describes it, a second underplot, one promised but one that never materializes in the course of the play, and this involves the small boy whom Clov sees outside the window. More of him later.

I take Hamm's "prayer"—he also forces his father to pray before giving him the promised sugarplum—as his personal celebration and definition of the artist. In the "old shelter," and alone against the silence, he first calls to his father (to his god) and then, reversing roles, becomes the father calling to his son (Christ?). There is no answer from either side. Hamm then retreats inward, but at the moment that he is seemingly alone he is not alone, but rather being "watched"—by a rat perhaps, by someone in the corridor (the "steps"). Surely he is being watched by us; it is inconceivable that an actor onstage can say that line ("I'm being watched") without the audience's silently affirming the truth, just as Hamlet's "Now I am alone" (which opens his speech contrasting the actor's tears as Hecuba with his own lack of passion to take revenge [2.2.554]) is contradicted by our presence.

Then Beckett's artist begins, leading first with words ("babble, babble") and following with the portrait of the imaginative efforts of a solitary child who turns himself into children, "two, three, so as to be together, and whisper together, in the dark." The effort is procreative, "patterning down, like the millet grains." Too optimistic, too close to an unqualified celebration of art as a public act challenging our solitude, Hamm cuts off the reverie with "Ah let's get it over." The playlet *Come and Go* seems to be anticipated here: the characters, two and then three, babbling together, needing each other, balancing their private fears with communal responses, and achieving a union with each other and with the audience at the end, this double union itself symbolized by the rings ("I can feel the rings"). At issue here is the bonds of language that at once define our separateness and yet are the human way of sharing our common isolation.

This celebration of art is not unqualified, however; the play is catholic in its complexity, in its ability to suspend antitheses without enforcing choice. For one thing, that communality with the audience and the move-ment from an outer to an inner world emerge only when form is given to decay, or when one "reality" is demolished so that an illusory "reality" of words and vision can be attempted—I stress *attempted*. More literally, we must sacrifice: bicycles to wheelchairs; real dogs to three-legged imitations; Flora and Pompona to a solitary, inner room; ideas and issues (such as raised by Mother Pegg, the Socratic figure, and the father who calls for Christian charity) to process itself; life, even as narrowly defined, to art; and past-oriented intellect to the experience of the immediate stage.

Hamm's inner world is not a comfortable one; indeed, it thrives only on tensions. He cannot shake off the curiosity to go outside his world; he wants to be near the window, to feel, to experience the elements (the light, the wind, the sound, and the smell of the sea) of physical reality. Near the end of the play Hamm feels cold and must be covered with a rug. Moreover, Clov leaves without obeying his master's orders. Physical life threatens this artifice at every moment, whether that life be as insignificant as a flea (which Hamm must promptly kill) or as significant as the small boy seen outside the window. Hamm has denied that boy in the past, in a story; he can refuse bread to his father. Yet the boy comes away, "a potential procreator." If the boy does exist outside, Hamm's hope is that he will die there. If he doesn't die, however, "he'll come here," Hamm argues, as his playwright's mind spins in circles of possibilities. If the end of the play is willed by Hamm, as the final ascension of the tragic character, the approach of the boy, conversely, forces that end upon him. As with government officials who "resign," we always wonder if they jumped or were pushed. Similarly, the flea's mere presence drives Hamm to desiring an escape on a raft, abandoning a ship threatened by an otherwise insignificant creature. Unlike the world of *Godot* with its blooming tree, there is even less celebration of meager life in *Endgame*. A father and a mother, however decrepit, are silenced as a new character, a potential procreator who is also an imagined destroyer, appears on the scene.

Like that of the radio plays, Hamm's blind world lacks even that physical verification known but rejected by the painter-engraver who went mad when he saw only ashes in his own three-dimensional creation. Even Clov observes that there are moments when his master hasn't "much conversation all of a sudden." His is an effort, a prolonged creative effort as much burden as achievement, to keep this inner world, this artifice, alive. Unlike Prospero, Hamm does not have the option of giving up his magic island for the reality of Naples, of abandoning his art by breaking his staff and drowning his magic book. If he "makes" an option by informing his suffering, he does so only by closing off the option for life, however ragged that physical existence is in Beckett when we think of all the impotent, maimed, decaying characters who inhabit his canvas. Something is taking its "course," and in this line we have, perhaps, the celebration of the artistic process itself, that unified artifice composed of actor and audience. Still, "course" sounds too close to "corpse" to leave us comfortable with any unqualified view of Beckett's portrait of the artist.

It cannot be otherwise. Art and life—no less—are at length a process, a fictive title given to what would otherwise be only an accumulation of seconds, of grains of sand. It is never the same pus from second to second, as Vladimir observes. Beckett seems concerned to record—to "chronicle," to use Hamm's word—that process. The issue is not, I think, whether he is being optimistic or pessimistic, or even whether *Endgame* is more "bleak" than *Godot*. Beckett is optimistic about art, *romantic,* as I have used that word, because without the process we would have only time, seconds, grain upon grain. Art, though, is not a thing but only a process; it is an imposition to make a little meaning, and therefore is better than nothing. The process of using words to talk about what is happening, about the way it is, about our days, whether we see them as happy days or as ones filled by lost ones—all is an imposition. Life is about dying—the Renaissance knew this well enough in their *ars moriendi* tradition—and about decaying; it is all downhill from the womb on. Play—child's play or the play of the legitimate theater—dares to give form to this irrefutable fact, thereby imitating the very life process that mocks any attempt at meaning, let alone stability in our existence. *Endgame* is, I think, more bold than bleak. The dead have nothing to say, to themselves or to us. The process of words and the imagination is compatible only with life, and hence the title of a more recent story by Beckett, "Imagination Dead Imagine."

V

These issues of art and the role of the playwright are focused, I believe, in two of Hamm's major speeches: one, the story of the man begging food for his son (a speech broken off and then taken up three times in *Endgame*); the other, Hamm's final speech in the play.

The story itself begins from the "outside" as a memory that has plagued Hamm, rather than as a response to the present action of *Endgame*. Like that of *Cascando,* the story here becomes inseparable from the telling, and Hamm's struggles with that telling echo the situation of *Cascando's* narrator, whose account of Woburn soon merges partially and then unmistakably with his own struggles as storyteller. It is the situation of the narrator/ narrated all over. The "invasion" of the old man is at one with the story's own invasion of Hamm's inner world in *Endgame*. Like the narrator in *Embers,* Hamm struggles for precision, for the right word, for the most accurate description of the surroundings ("a hundred by the anemometer" and then "zero by the hygrometer," and so on). The hyperconscious effort, however, may be only a façade to keep the subject separated from the teller, for we might ask, with Yeats, "How can we know the dancer from the dance?"

Thematically, the story also underscores that life force threatening Hamm's aesthetic world. The father demands not food for the mind or for an actor's part, but, literally, food for his son's stomach, the issue being not artistic creation but the preservation of basic life. In his refusal of that request, Hamm resembles a Pozzo, the landowner whose bounty goes no farther than himself. The issue is a dichotomy that, as in *Godot,* we know must ultimately dissolve: life (bread) versus art. The story itself is soon linked to events within *Endgame* when Hamm's own father asks for food for himself and Nell. An aesthetic life-bringer, Hamm is, paradoxically, a would-be death-bringer. Still, he cannot shake off the father's request; the story itself returns, like the Bolton-Holloway story in *Embers.* A compromise is offered: Hamm will hire the father as gardener (appropriately, a life-sustaining process).

The story still acts as an irritant to the artist, like the proverbial grain of sand within the oyster. In his responses Hamm mixes disgust with the father, pious rationalizations against charity, neurotic outbursts ("Get out of here and love one another! Lick your neighbor as yourself"), a mockery of the father's state ("Perhaps I could throw myself out on the floor"), and at last an identification with both father and son. As we have seen, he is both the father calling the son the son calling the father. Such identification leads to self-perception, his sense of being watched, and then to his glorious definition of the artist's process that I have examined earlier. Hamm, in effect, "absorbs" that outer story assaulting his inner world as he incorporates the consciences of his characters and thereby abandons the practiced indifference to life outside. Christ-like, he takes onto himself the roles of father and son and, once having done this, transfers a plea for life to a personal aesthetic plea. Hamm now recognizes his own isolation, his own need for mercy, for understanding, as well as the role of the artist in giving form to that request. He peoples his lonely world the way a child does with the imaginary playmates of his fantasy. The details of the story are changed, but its central issue, the dependency of each of us on an audience—literally, on someone to hear our plea or, thematically, someone to hear our words—remains unchanged.

The final appearance of the story demands that Clov, the actor, take the father's role, and this he does with a plaintive "Ah," much like Estragon's pathetic "Ah" in *Godot* when Vladimir reminds him of the object of their waiting. Once shared, the internalized story gives birth to Clov's own brief career as playwright, much to Hamm's displeasure, as we have seen, yet also delivered at Hamm's request. The futility of the art is also its glory, for the stories Hamm tries to divorce from himself, to pass off as external and as bearing no relation to his situation, turn on their outward trajectory and converge on their creator. The resulting art is, from a pessimist's perspective, an exercise in monomania; from a more optimistic reading, it is the painful, inevitable sharing of one's inner life. All along, Hamm was father and son: we have the missing author-character from Pirandello's *Six Characters in Search of an Author,* but here sufficient, not deficient; present, and not absent.

Despite its seeming chaos on the surface, Hamm's last speech, that string of short phrases and snatches of dialogue much like that of Winnie in *Happy Days,* provides the most sustained insight into his playwright's mentality. In the words of the Unnamable, it is the "end of the joke," the aesthetic painkiller, if you will, as handy as that literal painkiller in the cupboard was not. Unseen, except by us, Clov constitutes the onstage audience of one. The speech itself is surely meant to contrast with Hamm's opening dialogue: this time Hamm is not discovered but rather constitutes *all* the stage, at least as far as he knows, and the speech is about endings rather than beginnings. The proper verbal constructions, in terms of his opening lines, would be something akin to "Me to play having played." No fear of mere "reveling" here.

Hamm's speech seems to be madness without matter. As with the scattered fragments in the closing lines of Eliot's *The Waste Land,* however, there is here an order and a depth of reference below the surface. Clov is absent, though he stands impassive upstage. The sheet with which he "discovered" Hamm at the opening is now useless. In a larger sense, Hamm has been revealed, the play itself representing his disclosure as a symbol. The removal of the sheet itself is thereby the stimulus for an aesthetic revelation. He is now moving toward the purely symbolic, and the chess metaphor comes to the fore, chess itself a symbolic enactment of literal battles and armies: "Me to play" and "Old Endgame." Indeed, Hamm is moving toward the same sense of completeness found by Mr. Endon in *Murphy.* The King, the central piece, is now immobile at the center of the board, the word for both the theater and the field of chess pieces. Then "discard" the last life-support; the gaff is thrown away, though the dog, symbol of Hamm's artifice, is retained.

We see the artist now attempting to document the moment before human extinction. It is the process toward that movement, and not the actual event itself, defining the limits of our earthly inquiry.

Like Shakespeare, Beckett does not depict a hereafter. We may speculate on what will happen to Lear—can a pagan go to any sort of heaven?—but the Renaissance playwright, like the modern one, is content to show him approaching the end, promised or otherwise. There is a farewell here to the audience, obscene to be sure, and with that salute an identification with us as Hamm uses the plural possessive "our." The "You" who wants poetry, or the efficacy of prayer, or night to come is also the "you" that, in an absurdist or relative world, must cry in darkness. Again, we all die alone. Hamm's aesthetic consciousness, like that of the narrator in *Cascando,* is now most acute: "Nicely put, that."

If relativity, both in terms of time itself and the mutability of all human things, relentlessly moves on, Hamm, now enveloped in his story, is about to make time run, to echo the Renaissance poet Marvell. The time is "over, reckoning closed, and story ended." The wish for extinction, however, cannot hold as the life force, the final reference to the father and his starving son, is sounded. Hamm cannot shake off that memory. An invasion of his world, the story irritates the aesthetic fiber he has so closely woven. It is another world, with a past, with characters, and involving those issues of life and the sustenance of life that Hamm has otherwise so assiduously blocked out in his bomb shelter, in his circumscribed, lonely, inner world. The "Oh I put him before his responsibilities" sounds as much neurotic as convincing. Then with a *calm*—again, one of Beckett's favorite words— returning, Hamm reverses himself in the recognition that he is not alone, that he is part and parcel of all humanity, including us, including the fictive, or seemingly fictive father and his son: "Well, there we are, there I am, that's enough." This is something "truly," though the aesthetic inner world is itself in flux, only a momentary stay against reality, and yet Hamm will now be able to sustain this playwright-actor's posture at least until the end.

He approaches death with the same sense of "knowing" his story that several modern biblical scholars have attributed to Christ, an "actor" who plays the parts of a visitor to earth, prophet, crucified savior, and risen spirit. We approach now the closest thing to transcendence in Beckett, undercut, of course, by the fact that Hamm *"remains motionless"* as the curtain closes (he can no more leave his stage than Vladimir and Estragon can leave theirs). The dog is discarded, the last vestige of his creation; and then in a brilliant gesture he throws the whistle toward us, the audience—the *"auditorium."* Though the isolation is illusory—again, Clov is backstage, visible to us if not to Hamm—for Hamm it is a convincing illusion. He is approaching the nonbeing sought by Nell in her vision of a silent, white ocean bottom, an empty world where nothingness is a fact, not a conceit, where we can cease to be like those talkative "political" artists who, in giving form to nothing, are bound to fail. In essence, Hamm is trying to give up the last hold on life, even if that "life" be the illusory existence of the stage world.

The transcendence itself is aborted. However much he would later cut away at the time scheme or the plot or the place of his plays (witness *Breath*), Beckett cannot present us with nothing: "nothing" itself can be spoken of but not enacted. A bare stage is only a bare stage and not a play. Here Beckett is like Emily Dickinson in "I heard a fly buzz when I died," as she tries poetically to cross the thin boundary line between life and death and is frustrated in that attempt when a fly intervenes between her eyes and the "light." Beckett is trying to go to the nonstate, if I may put it that way, of nonbeing. That is the way Hamm would "play it," so that he could "speak no more about it." I repeat his wish: "speak no more." He seeks here not the failure of words, the very possibility that unnerves Winnie. Nor will he use words anymore to define nonbeing.

Now, without words and with the major character free of the tension in seeking physical life or death, we move to the level of mime. Our audience surrogate, the silent Clov, now sees Hamm hold the bloodied handkerchief before him and then cover his face. Two phrases act as glosses to the action. One is the descriptive "Old stauncher," lest an audience member fail to identify properly the symbol, Hamm's Greek-like mask that is the physical correlative for his misery, for his suffering than which no one's is greater, as he reminds us early in the play. In effect, Hamm, like the figures in Greek myths, has passed through earthly existence and literally become a star. He has won his right to be a symbol, a symbol sustained by the play, a symbol that now wordlessly compresses all that he means, or has meant. This wretched piece of a costume, in effect, now equals the entire play. In Beckett, truly, the last shall be first. One also thinks of the handkerchief worn by Keaton in *Film,* and that used by Willie in *Happy Days,* though neither was so developed, nor so perfect a symbol of suffering.

The other phrase, a tantalizing one, is the closing "You . . . remain." Initially, it appears simply an appositive for "Old stauncher," but I also take it as a reference to the audience. That is, Hamm has now *realized* his role; he has been elevated to a symbol. Our task has now just begun; we must leave the theater, refreshed by Beckett's mirror world, and must encounter the suffering anew. Outside of here it is hell, as the Beckett characters are fond of saying. We remain; we are the "mutes and audience" of the act to which Hamlet refers (5.2.337).

The play closes beyond words, as Hamm covers his face with the handkerchief and, like the Auditor in *Not I,* lowers his arms and in a mockery of mime and its movements stops on the stage direction to remain *"motionless."* Initiated by language, the play ends in silence, the *"Brief tableau,"* like that called for by Beckett in *The Unnamable. Curtain.* It will also start again; as Winnie observes, even if the glass breaks, it will be there whole tomorrow. Tomorrow the handkerchief will revert to the old sheet covering Hamm, that, with the blood-stained handkerchief, will in turn be removed, discovering another potential tragic hero—or "figure," if "hero" sounds too affirmative for some readers. The uncovering will allow theatrical life to flow again, the act of artistic creation, the long creative process to which Hamm himself refers, the informing of a vision and the production of a symbol—a symbol that, at the end, will remain with us, only to be undone the next day, the next performance. Curtain. . . .

Chronology

1906	Born Good Friday, April 13, at Foxrock, near Dublin, second son of William and Mary Beckett.
1919–23	Attends Potora Royal School at Enniskillen, County Fermanagh (Oscar Wilde's school).
1923–27	Attends Trinity College, Dublin; B.A. in French and Italian.
1928	Begins two-year fellowship at Ecole Normale Supérieure in Paris. Friendship with Joyce begins, as does immersion in the work of Descartes.
1929	Early writings in *Transition*. Defends Joyce's *Finnegans Wake* in the essay "Dante . . . Bruno. Vico . . . Joyce."
1930	*Whoroscope*.
1931	Returns to Trinity College as lecturer in French and takes M.A. *Proust*, and *Le Kid*, parody of Corneille.
1932	Resigns post as lecturer. Writes unpublished *Dream of Fair to Middling Women*.
1933	Death of William Beckett. Begins three years in London.
1934	*More Pricks Than Kicks*.
1936	Travels in Germany. *Echo's Bones*.
1937	Returns to Paris.
1938	Sustains serious stab wound from stranger. Begins relationship with Suzanne Dumesnil. *Murphy*.
1939	Returns to Paris after Irish sojourn.
1940	Is active in French Resistance movement.
1942	Flees to unoccupied France to escape Gestapo. Works as day laborer for two years in farming. Writes *Watt*.
1945	Goes to Ireland after German surrender. Returns to France for service with Irish Red Cross. Returns to Paris permanently.
1946–50	Productive period of writing in French, including the trilogy *Molloy, Malone meurt,* and *L'Innommable,* and the play, *En attendant Godot*.

1947   *Murphy* published in French.

1950   Visits Ireland at the time of his mother's death.

1951   *Molloy* published. *Malone meurt* published.

1952   *Godot* published.

1953   First performance of *Godot* in Paris. *Watt* published. *L'Innommable* published.

1955   *Waiting for Godot* opens in London.

1956   *Waiting for Godot* opens in Miami, Florida, for first American performance.

1957   *All That Fall* broadcast by BBC. *Fin de Partie* published. French first performance in London.

1958   *Krapp's Last Tape* and *Endgame* (in English) open in London.

1959   *Embers* broadcast by BBC. Honorary degree from Trinity College, Dublin.

1960   *Krapp's Last Tape* produced in Paris as *La Dernière Bande*.

1961   *Comment c'est* published. *Happy Days* opens in New York City. Shares, with Borges, International Publishers' Prize.

1962   Marries Suzanne Dumesnil, March 25. *Words and Music* broadcast by BBC.

1963   *Comédie* first performed in Ulm, Germany, and in London and Paris as *Play* in 1964. *Cascando* broadcast in Paris.

1964   Goes to New York City to help produce his *Film* (with Buster Keaton).

1966   *Eh Joe,* a television play. *Come and Go,* a "dramaticule."

1969   Nobel Prize in Literature. *Breath.*

1972   *The Lost Ones. Not I* performed in New York, and later in London (1973).

1975   Beckett's production of *Warten auf Godot* at the Schiller-Theater, Berlin.

1976   *Ends and Odds; Fizzles; All Strange Away. Footfalls* premieres in London.

1977   *Ghost Trio* and . . . *but the clouds* . . . (a television play). *Collected Poems in English and French.*

1978   *Mirlitonnades* (35 short poems).

1980   *Company; One Evening.*

1981   *Ill Seen Ill Said; Rockaby. Quad,* a mime play.

1983   *Catastrophe. Worstward Ho.*

Contributors

HAROLD BLOOM, Sterling Professor of the Humanities at Yale University, is the author of *The Anxiety of Influence, Poetry and Repression,* and many other volumes of literary criticism. His forthcoming study, *Freud: Transference and Authority,* attempts a full-scale reading of all of Freud's major writings. A MacArthur Prize Fellow, he is general editor of five series of literary criticism published by Chelsea House. During 1987–88, he served as Charles Eliot Norton Professor of Poetry at Harvard University.

THEODOR W. ADORNO was the central figure in the Frankfurt School of Criticism. His major works include *Negative Dialectics* and *The Philosophy of Modern Music.*

HUGH KENNER, Professor Emeritus of English at The Johns Hopkins University, is the leading critic of the High Modernists (Pound, Eliot, Joyce) and of Beckett. His books include *The Pound Era* and *The Stoic Comedians.*

ANTONY EASTHOPE teaches at the University of Kansas.

STANLEY CAVELL is a Professor of Philosophy at Harvard University. He is the author of *The Claims of Reason, The Senses of Walden, Must We Mean What We Say?,* and *Themes out of School: Effects and Causes.*

RICHARD GILMAN is Professor of Drama at Yale University. His books include *The Confusion of Realms, Common and Uncommon Masks,* and *The Making of Modern Drama.* He has been literary editor for *The New Republic* and drama critic for *Commonweal* and *Newsweek.*

PAUL LAWLEY is Tutor in the Department of English and Comparative Studies at the University of Warwick. He also works in a tutorial capacity for the Open University.

RUBY COHN is a Professor of Comparative Literature at the University of

California at Davis and has written extensively on drama. Her works include *Dialogue in American Drama, Currents in American Drama, Modern Shakespeare Offshoots,* and on Beckett, *Samuel Beckett: The Comic Gamut, Back to Beckett,* and *Just Play: Beckett's Theater.*

SIDNEY HOMAN teaches in the English Department at the University of Florida. He has written extensively on Shakespeare and his *Beckett's Theaters: Interpretations for Performance* won the Bucknell University Press Award.

Bibliography

Alvarez, Alfred. *Beckett.* London: Fontana, 1973.

Bair, Dierdre. *Samuel Beckett: A Biography.* New York: Harcourt Brace Jovanovich, 1978.

Baldwin, Helen Louise. *Samuel Beckett's Real Silence.* University Park: Pennsylvania State University Press, 1981.

Ben-Zvi, Linda. "Samuel Beckett, Fritz Mauthner, and the Limits of Language." *PMLA* 95 (1980): 183–200.

Blanchot, Maurice. *Le Livre à venir,* 256–60. Paris: Gallimard, 1959.

Bloom, Harold, ed. *Modern Critical Views: Samuel Beckett.* New York: Chelsea House, 1985.

Brater, Enoch. *Beckett at Eighty: Beckett in Context.* New York: Oxford University Press, 1986.

Bruck, Jan. "Beckett, Benjamin, and the Modern Crisis in Communication." *New German Critique* no. 26 (1982): 159–72.

Butler, Lance St. John. *Samuel Beckett and the Meaning of Being: A Study in Literature as Philosophy.* London: Macmillan, 1984.

Chevigny, Bell Gale, ed. *Twentieth-Century Interpretations of* Endgame: *A Collection of Critical Essays.* Englewood Cliffs, N.J.: Prentice-Hall, 1969.

Coe, Robert. *Beckett.* New York: Grove, 1964.

Cohn, Ruby. *Back to Beckett.* Princeton: Princeton University Press, 1973.

———. *Just Play: Beckett's Theatre.* Princeton: Princeton University Press, 1980.

———. *Samuel Beckett: The Comic Gamut.* New Brunswick, N.J.: Rutgers University Press, 1962.

Dearlove, J. E. *Accommodating the Chaos: Samuel Beckett's Nonrelational Art.* Durham, N.C.: Duke University Press, 1982.

Doherty, Francis. *Samuel Beckett.* London: Hutchinson University Library, 1971.

Driver, Tom F. "Beckett by the Madeleine." *Columbia University Forum* 4, no. 3 (1961): 21–25.

Duckworth, Colin. *Angels of Darkness: Dramatic Effects in Samuel Beckett with Special Reference to Eugene Ionesco.* London: Allen & Unwin, 1972.

Eastman, Richard. "The Strategy of Samuel Beckett's *Endgame.*" *Modern Drama* 2 (1959): 36–44.

Eliopulos, James. *Samuel Beckett's Dramatic Language.* The Hague: Mouton, 1975.

Esslin, Martin. *Meditations: Essays on Brecht, Beckett and the Media*. New York: Grove, 1984.

———. *The Theatre of the Absurd*. New York: Doubleday/Anchor, 1961.

———, ed. *Samuel Beckett: A Collection of Critical Essays*. Englewood Cliffs, N.J.: Prentice-Hall, 1965.

Fletcher, John. *Beckett, A Study of His Plays*. London: Methuen, 1972.

———. *Samuel Beckett's Art*. London: Chatto & Windus, and New York: Barnes & Noble, 1967.

Gassner, John. *Theatre at the Crossroads*, 256–61. New York: Holt, Rinehart & Winston, 1960.

Gontarski, S. E. *The Intent of Undoing in Samuel Beckett's Dramatic Texts*, 42–54. Bloomington: Indiana University Press, 1985.

———, ed. *On Beckett: Essays and Criticism*. New York: Grove, 1986.

Grayer, Lawrence, and Raymond Federman, eds. *Samuel Beckett: The Critical Heritage*. London: Routledge & Kegan Paul, 1979.

Grossvogel, David. *Four Playwrights and a Postscript: Brecht, Ionesco, Beckett, Genet*. Ithaca, N.Y.: Cornell University Press, 1962.

———. *The Self-Conscious Stage in Modern French Drama*. New York: Columbia University Press, 1961

Guicharnaud, Jacques (with June Beckelman). *Modern French Theatre from Giraudoux to Beckett*. New Haven: Yale University Press, 1961.

Harvey, Lawrence E. *Samuel Beckett: Poet and Critic*. Princeton, N.J.: Princeton University Press, 1970.

Hassan, Ihab Habib. *The Literature of Silence, Henry Miller and Samuel Beckett*. New York: Knopf, 1967.

Hasselbach, Hans-Peter. "*Samuel Beckett's Endgame: A Structural Analysis*." *Modern Drama* 19 (1976): 25–35.

Hayman, Ronald. *Samuel Beckett*. New York: Ungar, 1973.

Hesla, David H. *The Shape of Chaos, An Interpretation of the Art of Samuel Beckett*. Minneapolis: University of Minnesota Press, 1971.

Hoffman, Frederic John. *Samuel Beckett: The Language of Self*. Carbondale: Southern Illinois University Press, 1962.

Homan, Sidney. *Beckett's Theaters: Interpretations for Performance*. Lewisburg, Pa.: Bucknell University Press, 1954.

Iser, Wolfgang. "The Art of Failure: The Stifled Laugh in Beckett's Theatre." *Bucknell Review* 26, no. 1 (1981): 139–89.

Kenner, Hugh. *A Reader's Guide to Beckett*. New York: Farrar, Straus & Giroux, 1973.

———. *Samuel Beckett, A Critical Study*. Berkeley: University of California Press, 1968.

———. *The Stoic Comedians: Flaubert, Joyce and Beckett*. Berkeley: University of California Press, 1962.

Kern, Edith. *The Absolute Comic*. New York: Columbia University Press, 1980.

Knowlson, James. *Light and Darkness in the Theatre of Samuel Beckett*. London: Turret, 1972.

Kott, Jan. "*King Lear* or *Endgame*." Translated by Boleslaw Taborski. *Evergreen Review* 8, no. 33 (1964): 53–65. Reprinted in *Shakespeare Our Contemporary*. Garden City, N.Y.: Doubleday, 1964.

Lyons, Charles R. *Samuel Beckett*. London: Macmillan, 1983.

Mercier, Vivian. *Beckett/Beckett*. New York: Oxford University Press, 1977.

Mayoux, Jean-Jacques. "The Drama of Samuel Beckett." *Perspective* 11, no. 3 (1959): 142–55.

Morot-Sir, Edouard, Howard Harper, and Dougald McMillan, eds. *Samuel Beckett: The Art of Rhetoric*. Chapel Hill: University of North Carolina Press, 1976.

Pronko, Leonard Cabell. *Avant-Garde: The Experimental Theatre in France*. Berkeley and Los Angeles: University of California Press, 1962.

Riggs, Larry W. "Slouching toward Consciousness: Destruction of the Spectator-Role in *En attendant Godot* and *Fin de partie*." *Degré Second* 7 (1983): 57–79.

Robbe-Grillet, Alain. "Samuel Beckett, or 'Presence' in the Theatre." In Martin Esslin, ed. *Samuel Beckett: A Collection of Critical Essays*. Englewood Cliffs, N.J.: Prentice-Hall, 1965.

Rosen, Steven J. *Samuel Beckett and the Pessimistic Tradition*. New Brunswick, N.J.: Rutgers University Press, 1976.

Schneider, Alan. *Entrances: An American Director's Journey*. New York: Viking, 1986.

Schwab, Gabriele. "The Dialectic of Opening and Closing in Samuel Beckett's *Endgame*." *Yale French Studies*, no. 67 (1984): 191–202.

Shenker, Israel. "Moody Man of Letters." *The New York Times*, 6 May 1956.

Sherzer, Dina. "Beckett's *Endgame*, or What Talk Can Do." *Modern Drama* 22 (1978): 291–303.

Simpson, Alan. *Beckett and Behan, and a Theatre in Dublin*. London: Routledge & Kegan Paul, 1962.

Spurling, John and John Fletcher. *Beckett the Playwright*. New York: Hill & Wang, 1985.

Suvin, Darko. "Beckett's Purgatory of the Individual." *Tulane Drama Review* 11, no. 4 (1967): 23–36.

Weales, Gerald. "The Language of *Endgame*." *Tulane Drama Review* 6, no. 4 (1962): 107–117.

Webb, Eugene. *The Plays of Samuel Beckett*. Seattle: University of Washington Press, 1972.

Acknowledgments

"Trying to Understand *Endgame*" by Theodor W. Adorno from *New German Critique* 26 (Summer 1982), © 1982 by *New German Critique*. Reprinted by permission of *New German Critique*.

"Life in the Box" by Hugh Kenner from *Samuel Beckett: A Critical Study* by Hugh Kenner, © 1961, 1968 by Hugh Kenner. Reprinted by permission of the University of California Press.

"Hamm, Clov, and Dramatic Method in *Endgame*" by Antony Easthope from *Modern Drama* 10, no. 4 (February 1968), © 1968 by A. C. Edwards. Reprinted by permission.

"Ending the Waiting Game: A Reading of Beckett's *Endgame*" (originally entitled "Ending the Waiting Game") by Stanley Cavell from *Must We Mean What We Say* by Stanley Cavell, © 1969 by Stanley Cavell, © 1976 by Cambridge University Press. Reprinted by permission of Cambridge University Press.

"Beckett" by Richard Gilman from *The Making of Modern Drama* by Richard Gilman, © 1972, 1973, 1974 by Richard Gilman. Reprinted by permission of the author and Farrar, Straus & Giroux, Inc.

"Symbolic Structure and Creative Obligation in *Endgame*" by Paul Lawley from *Journal of Beckett Studies* 5 (Autumn 1979), © 1979 by the *Journal of Beckett Studies*. Reprinted by permission of John Calder Publishers Ltd.

"The Play That Was Rewritten: *Fin de partie*" by Ruby Cohn from *Just Play: Beckett's Theater* by Ruby Cohn, © 1980 by Princeton University Press. Reprinted by permission of Princeton University Press.

"*Endgame*: The Playwright Completes Himself" by Sidney Homan from *Beckett's Theaters: Interpretations for Performance* by Sidney Homan, © 1984 by Associated University Presses, Inc. Published by Bucknell University Press and reprinted by permission of Associated University Presses, Inc.

Index

157